Charles Mayton

Two-Step

TABLE OF CONTENTS

Foreword

by Blake Rayne

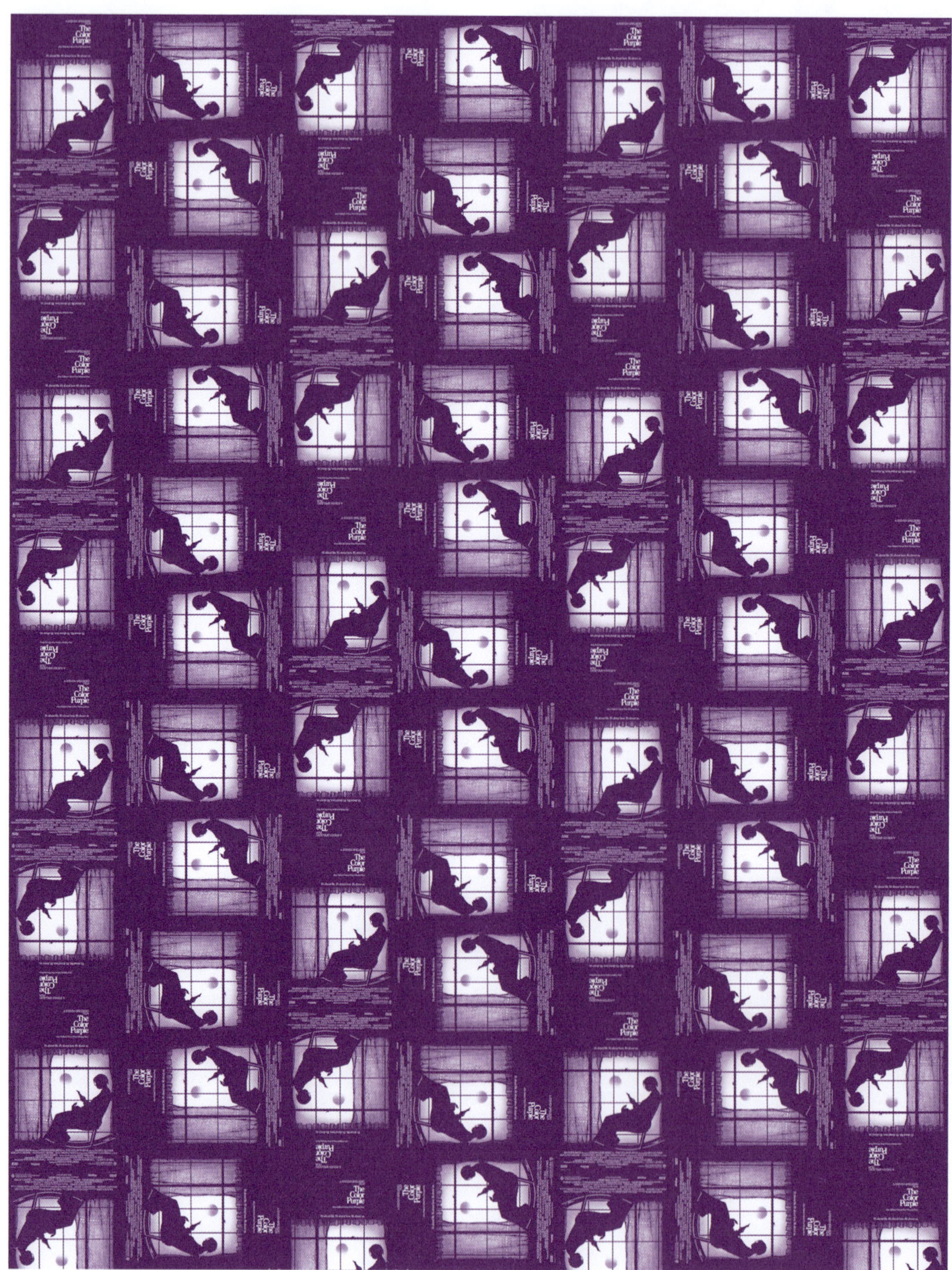

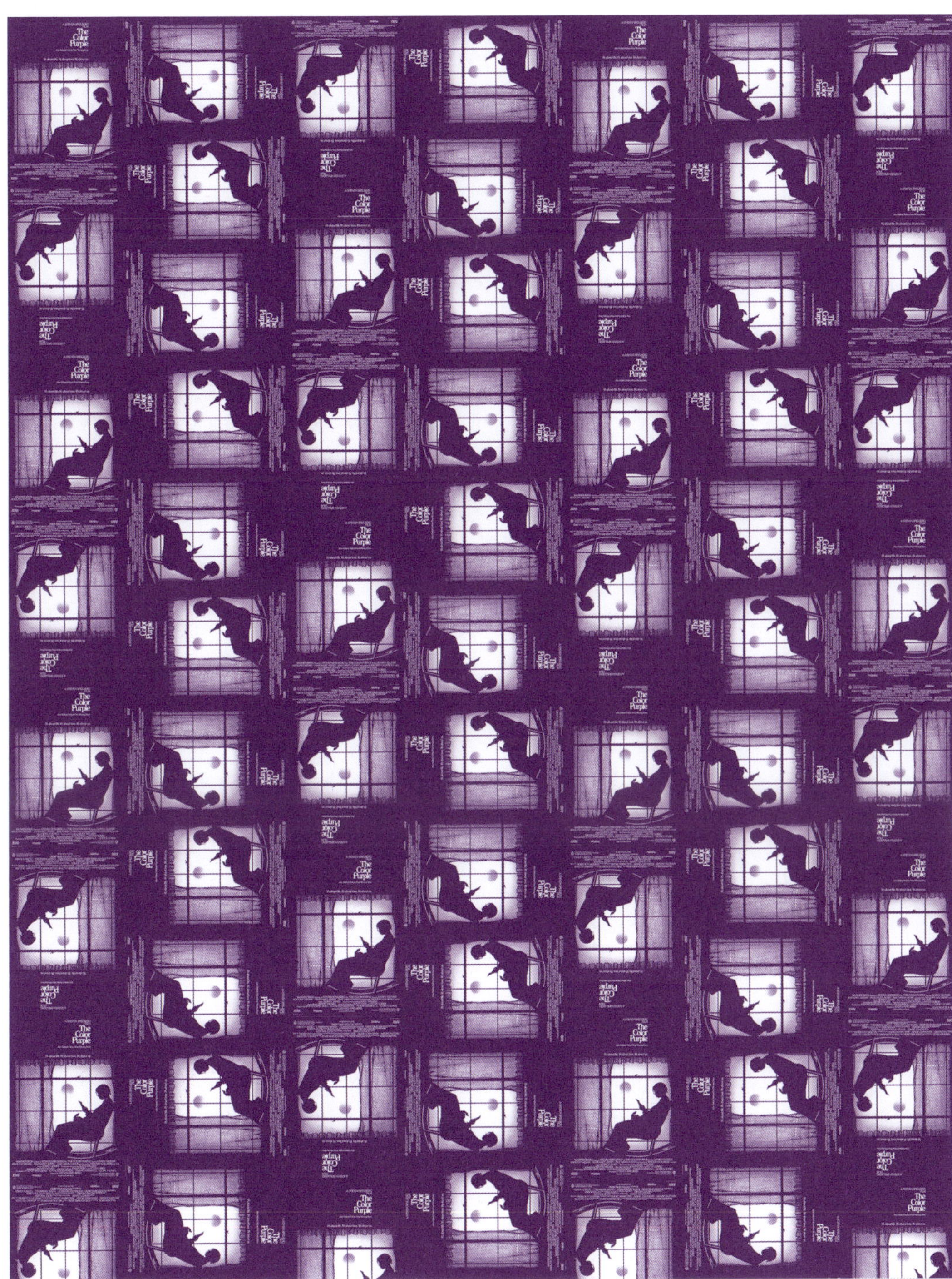

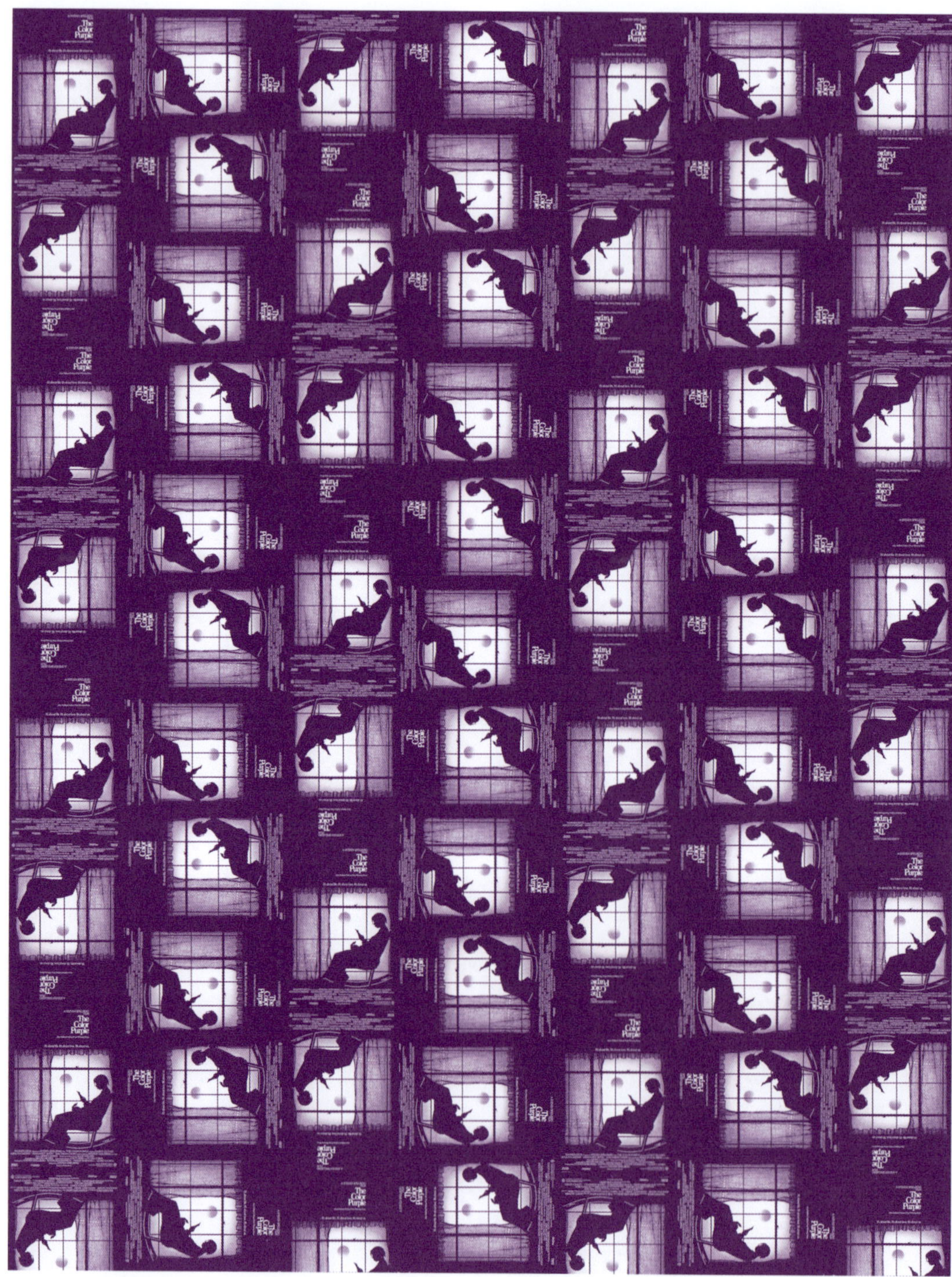

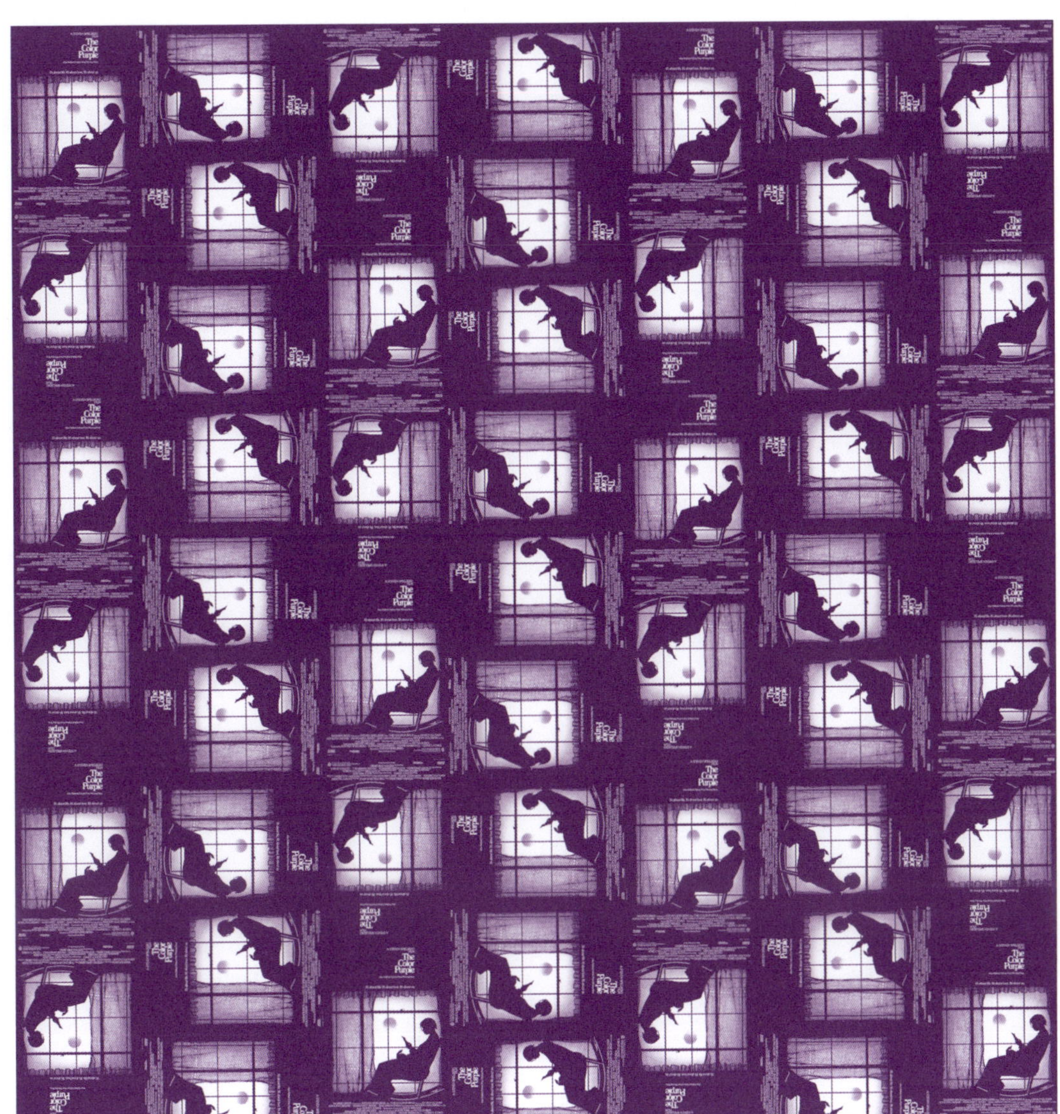

L

Charles Mayton's Allegory of Painting

by David Lewis

Allegory of Painting.
"In 1980, a serial killer popularly nicknamed the Tooth Fairy stalks and murders seemingly random families during sequential full moons.

He is nicknamed the Tooth Fairy due to his tendency to bite his victims' bodies, the uncommon size and sharpness of his teeth and other apparent oral fixations.

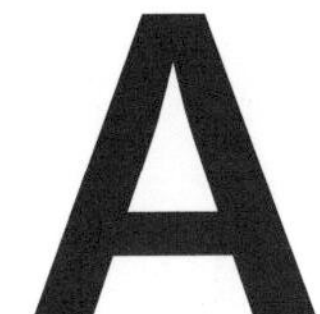

A

The Tooth Fairy is revealed to be a St. Louis film processing technician named Francis Dolarhyde.

He is a disturbed individual who is obsessed with the William Blake painting *The Great Red Dragon* and the *Woman Clothed with the Sun.*

Dolarhyde is unable to control his violent, sexual urges and believes that murdering people—or 'changing' them, as he calls it— allows him to more fully become an alternate personality he calls the 'Great Red Dragon,' after the

dominant character in Blake's painting."

Jeffrey Weiss on Jasper Johns. "The small *Painting Bitten by a Man*, also from 1961, is perhaps Johns's single most startling work and surely one of the most remarkable objects in the history of art since mid-century.

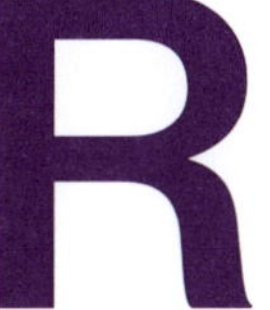

It is composed of a thick field of yellow-grey encaustic—on canvas mounted on a wood type plate—that has been aggressively violated (both by a body and as a body). Left behind is a hollow bearing tracks from the scraping action of the artist's teeth."

Bartholomew Ryan on Charles Mayton. "On a recent visit to Charles Mayton's studio, I was struck by a work titled *Trolling with a Tasteful Palette* (2012),[p. 43] in which a silhouette of a painter's palette, partially cropped, is suspended in a field of large and appealingly colorful, abstract brushstrokes.

A horizon line divides this immersive abstraction from the painting's upper portion of blank, primed canvas. It resembles a fish swimming in water— a playfulness that the title supports.

What I like about this painting is the quality of the fish / palette, almost cartoonish in its contours, and then the analogy between painting / sea and fishing / composition that the work sets up.

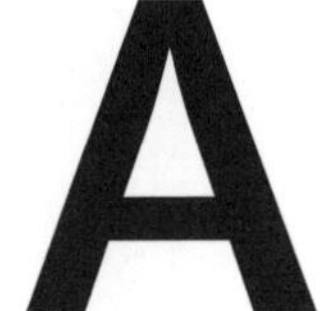

If, as many critics observe, painters today are drowning in the precedents set by art history, then Mayton here faces that weight head-on. In my dreams, the palette / fish speaks to me and says, 'Please don't eat me.'"

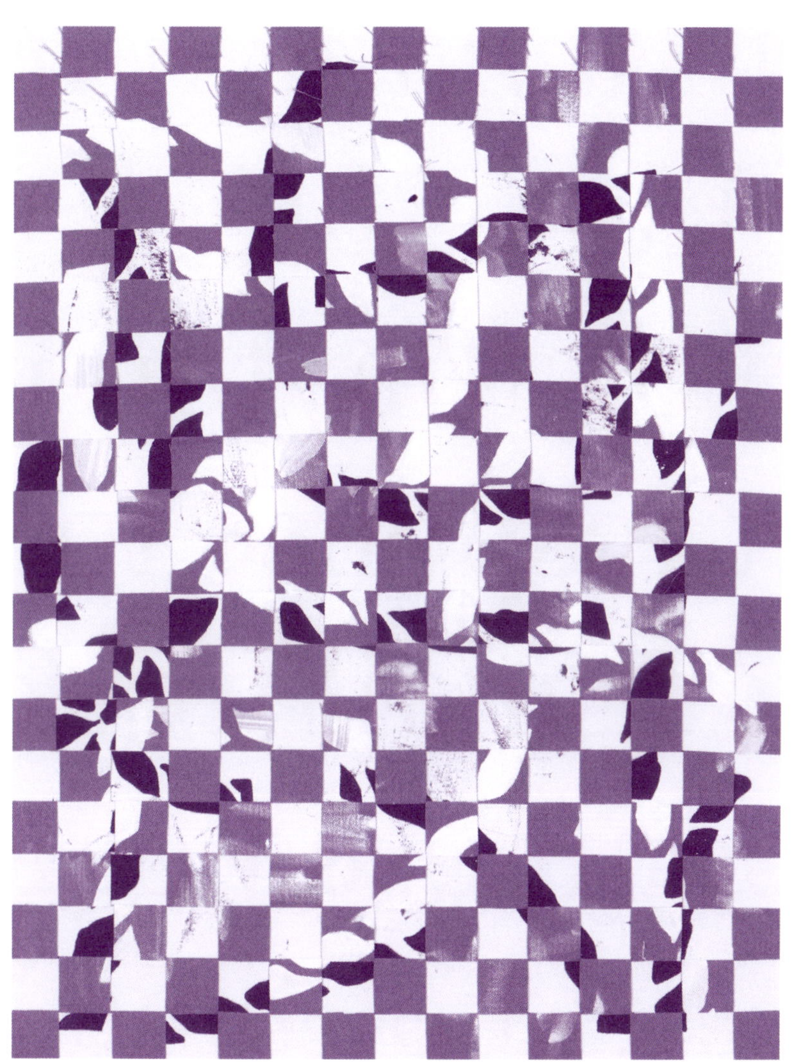

Charles Mayton with Jasper Johns: The small *Painting Eaten by a Man* (2012)[p. 75] was made by Mayton in direct response to Johns's small work. It is composed of a thick field of blue latex on which is mounted an empty sardine tin.

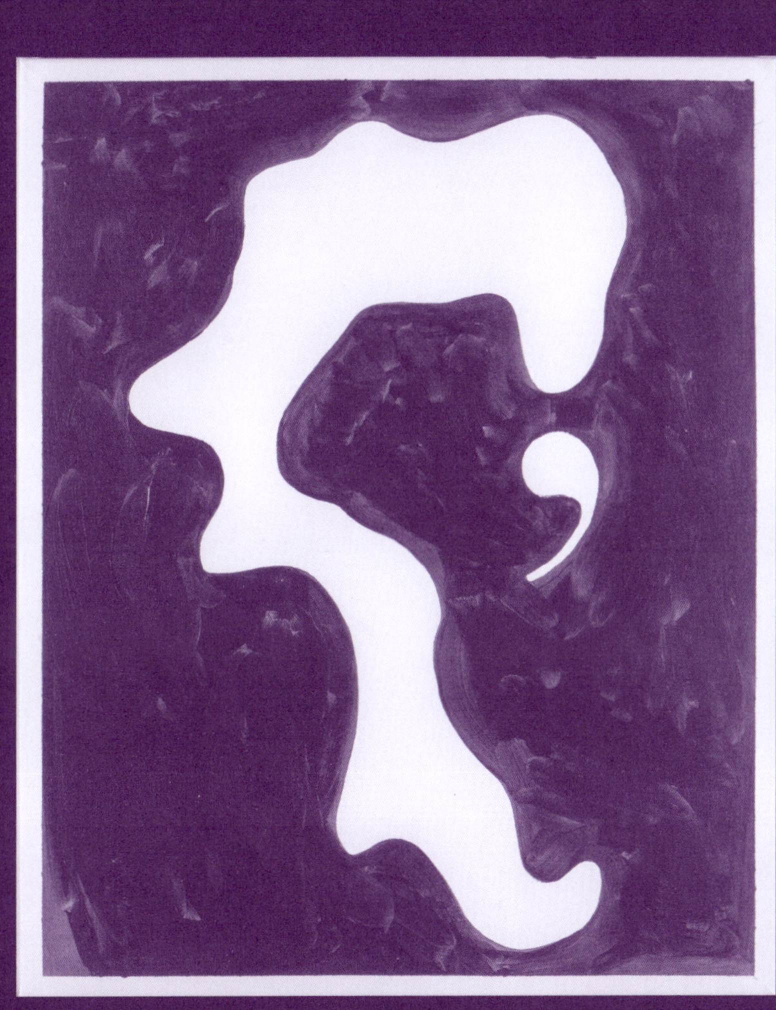

T

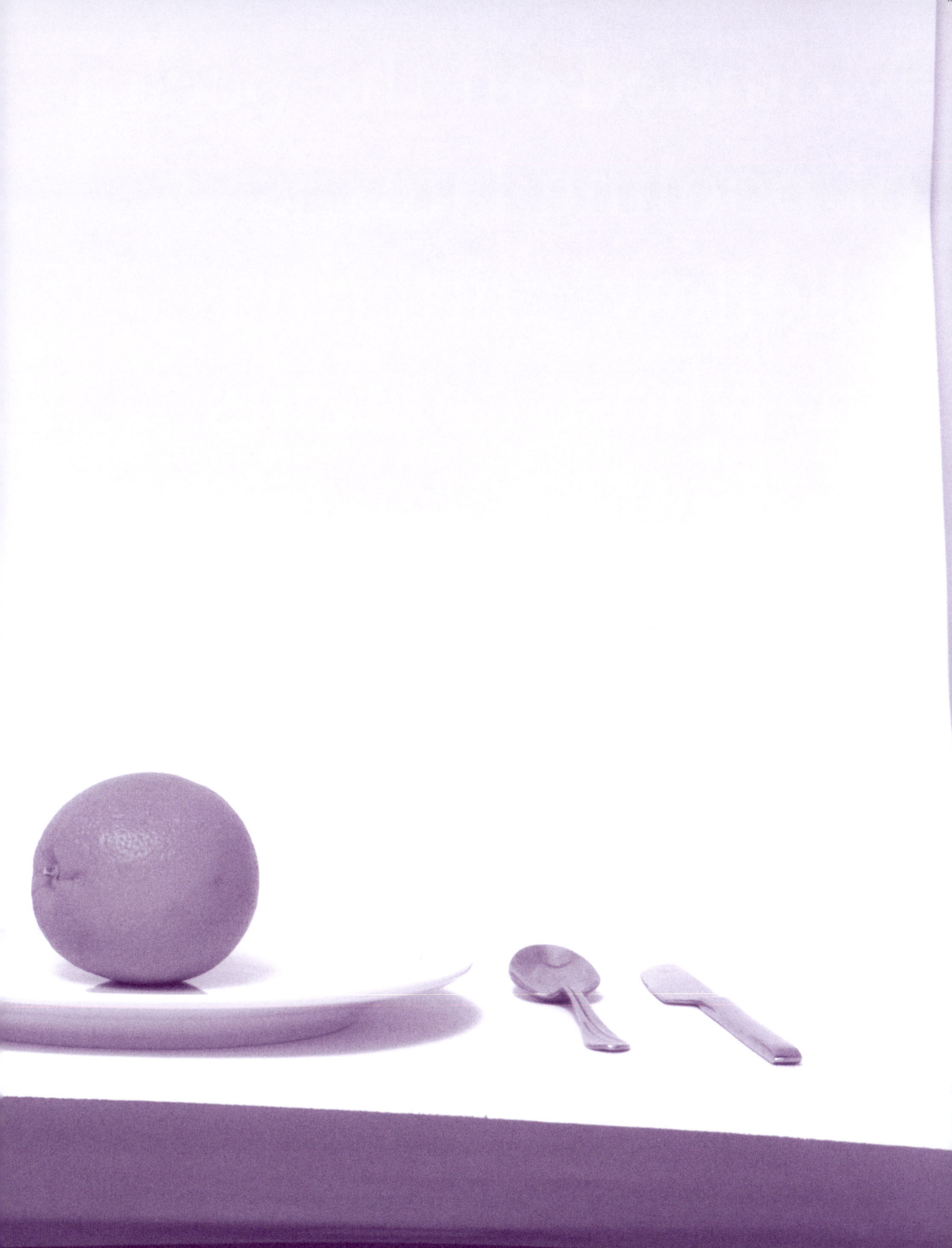

Mounted on the ocean
of pooling latex is
a hollow, glittering
tin, whose contents
presumably have been
reduced to chewable
slivers by the grinding
action of someone's
teeth.

This is a story about language. Can one "eat" words? If Johns is Mayton's true Penelope (or rather—assuming there is no objection to the double transmigration of souls—if he figures as Spencer to Dryden's Chaucer) then

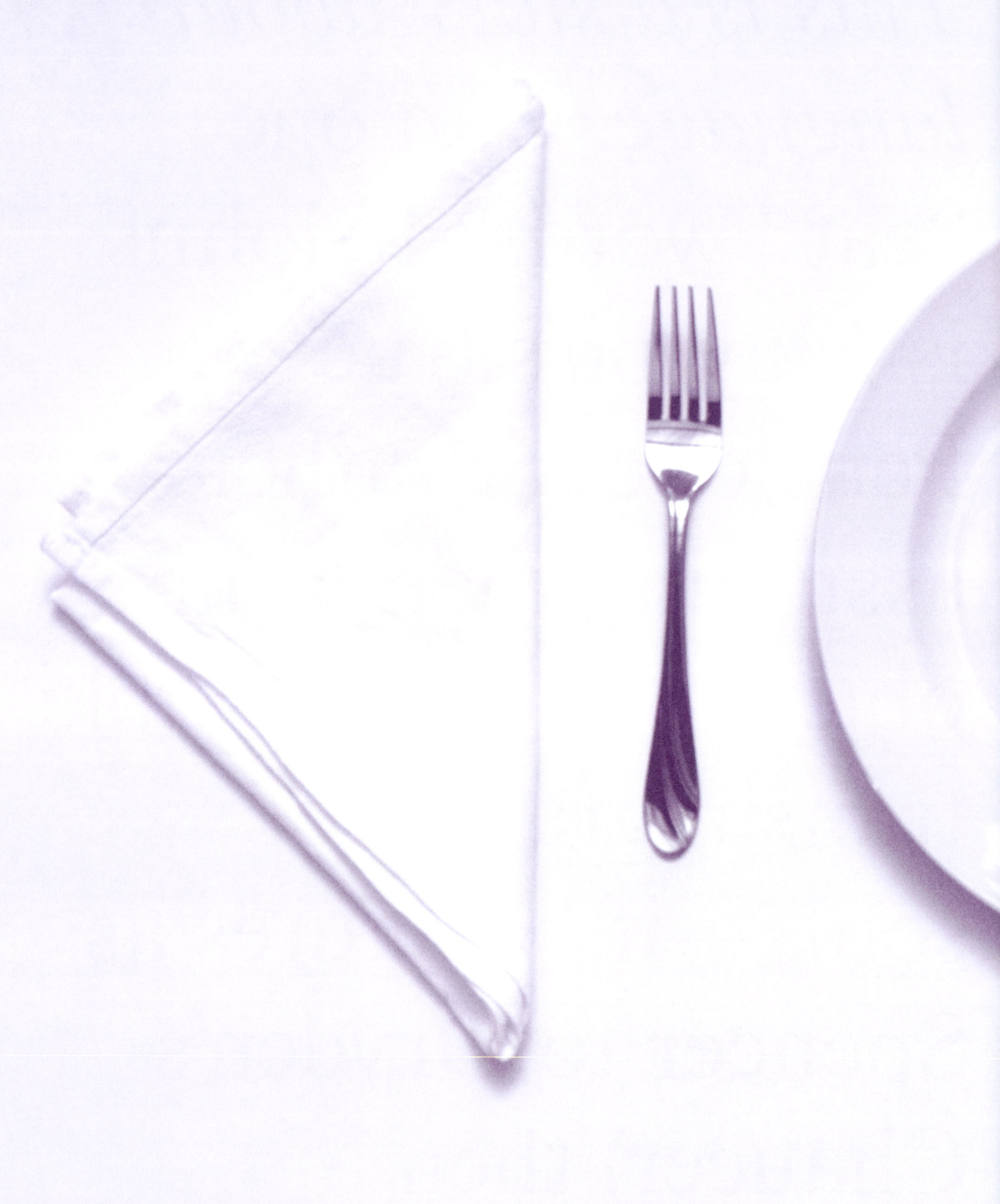

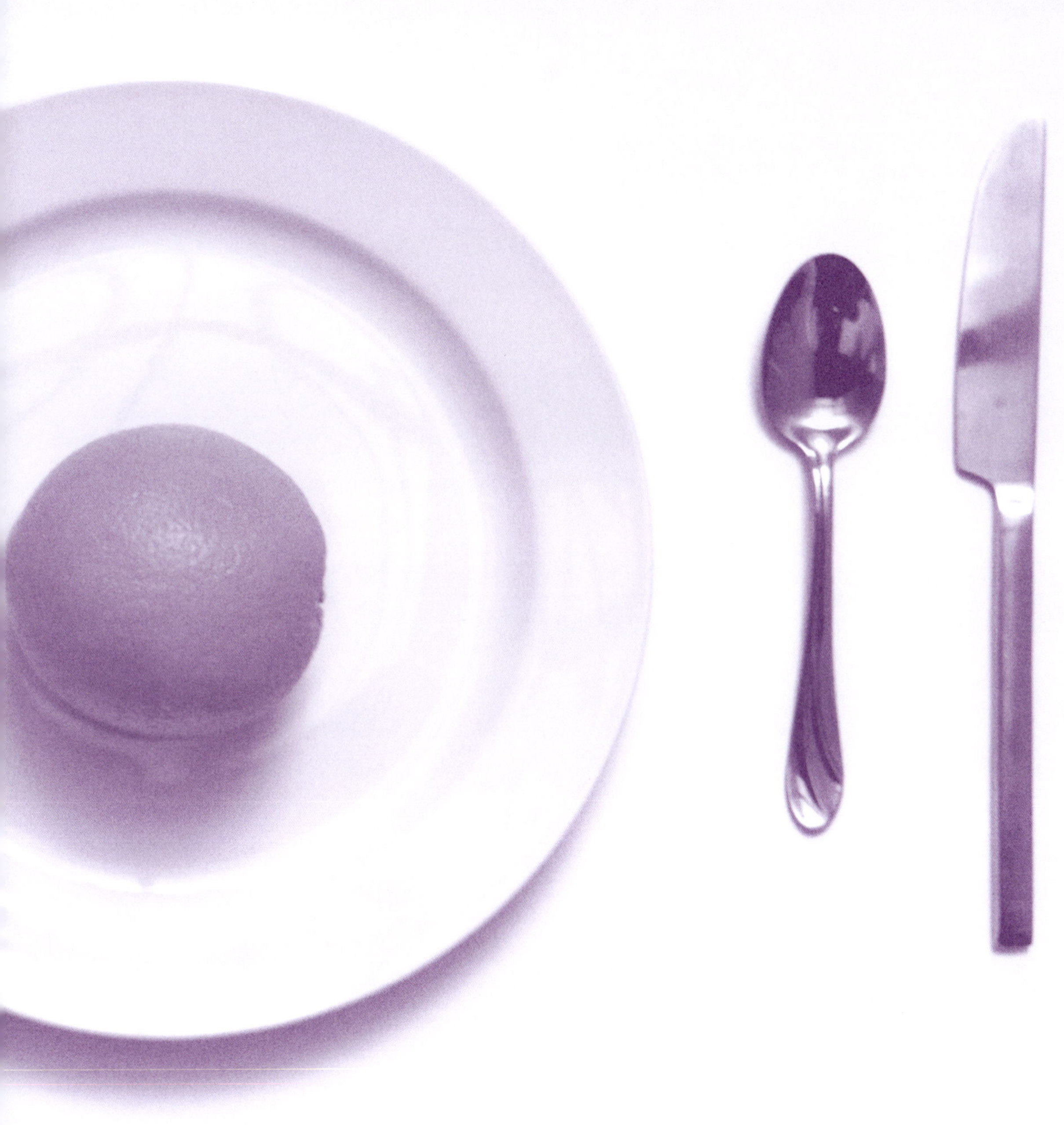

René Magritte is his first crowned cannibal king. Both antecedents yield the same inheritance, though: linguistic painting, structuralist painting, painting of and about signs.

And in all three cases, painting, however serene, is always holding something monstrous—that hatched and hungry serpent—at bay.

Ryan, again. The Sea, the Sea. "One way not to be eaten is to eat, and Mayton consumes painting's history, repurposing it in motifs and themes that run through his work.

He is fascinated
by René Magritte,
René Daniëls, Jasper
Johns, and others who
explore the potential of
language as something
linked to visual
symbols and signs.

For his first gallery show in New York, Mayton translated Magritte's famous *The Difficult Crossing* (1926)[p.99] in three dimensions within the space of the exhibition."

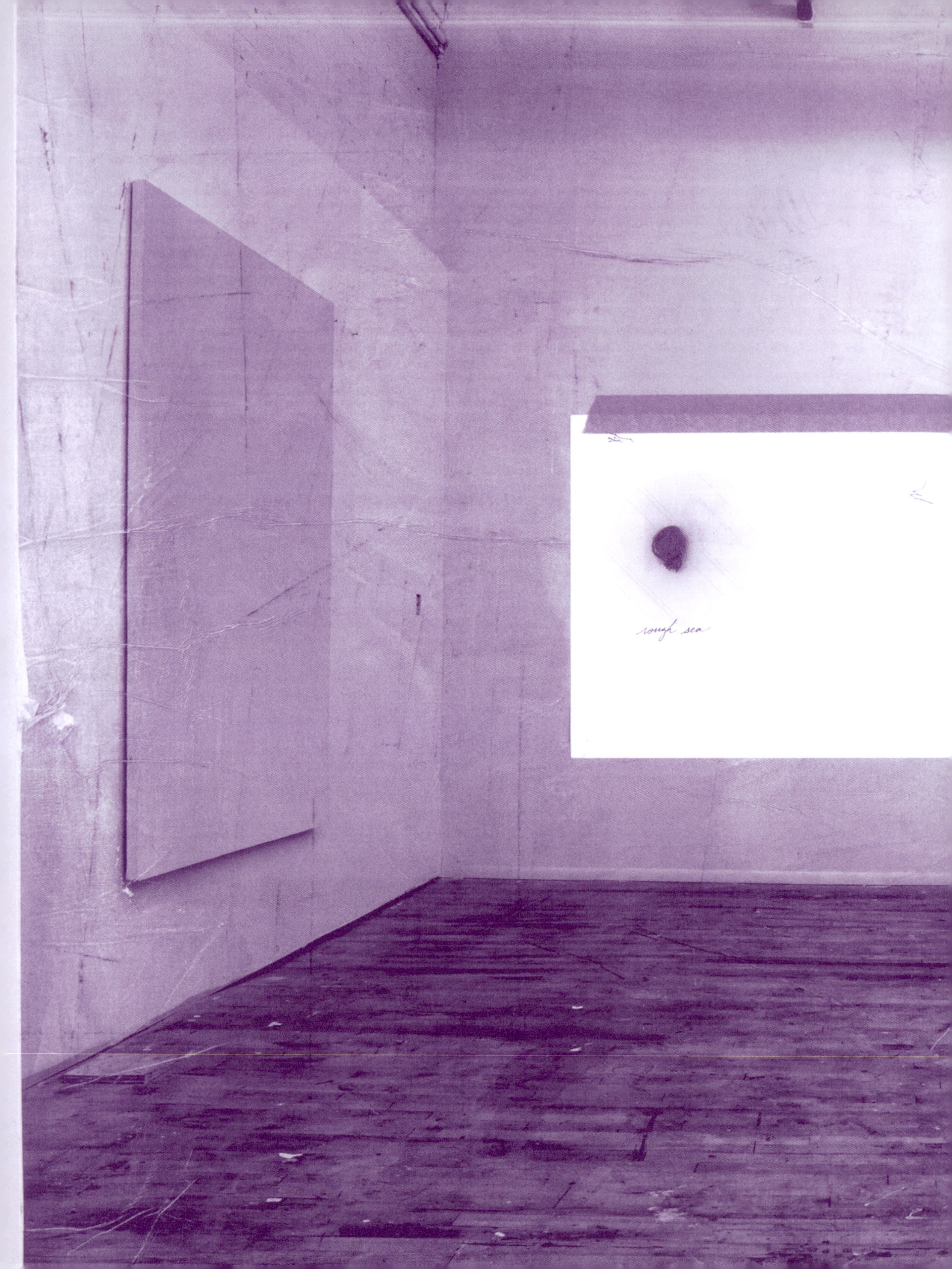
rough sea

Mayton with Magritte: The Rough Sea.^{p.68} The painting, which plays a game with the painting-within-Magritte's *The Difficult Crossing,*^{p.99} is, in fact, a photograph of the artist's studio. The studio is empty except for the blank canvases on the left and right walls. On the rear wall, however, is a photograph taped to the surface. It seems like a work hung in the fictional space of the empty studio: a painting-within-a-painting, like that on the same wall in Magritte's painting.

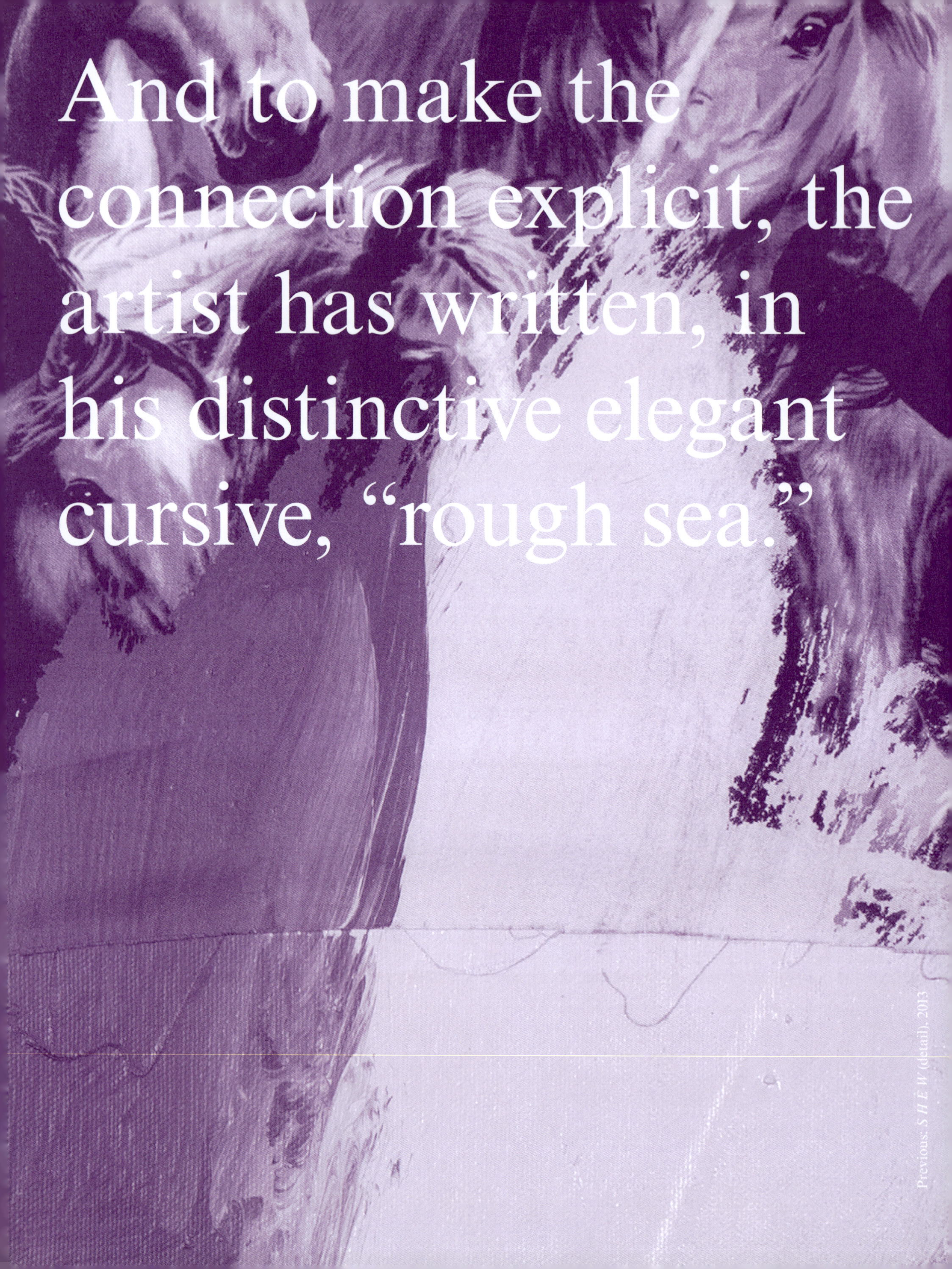

And to make the connection explicit, the artist has written, in his distinctive elegant cursive, "rough sea."

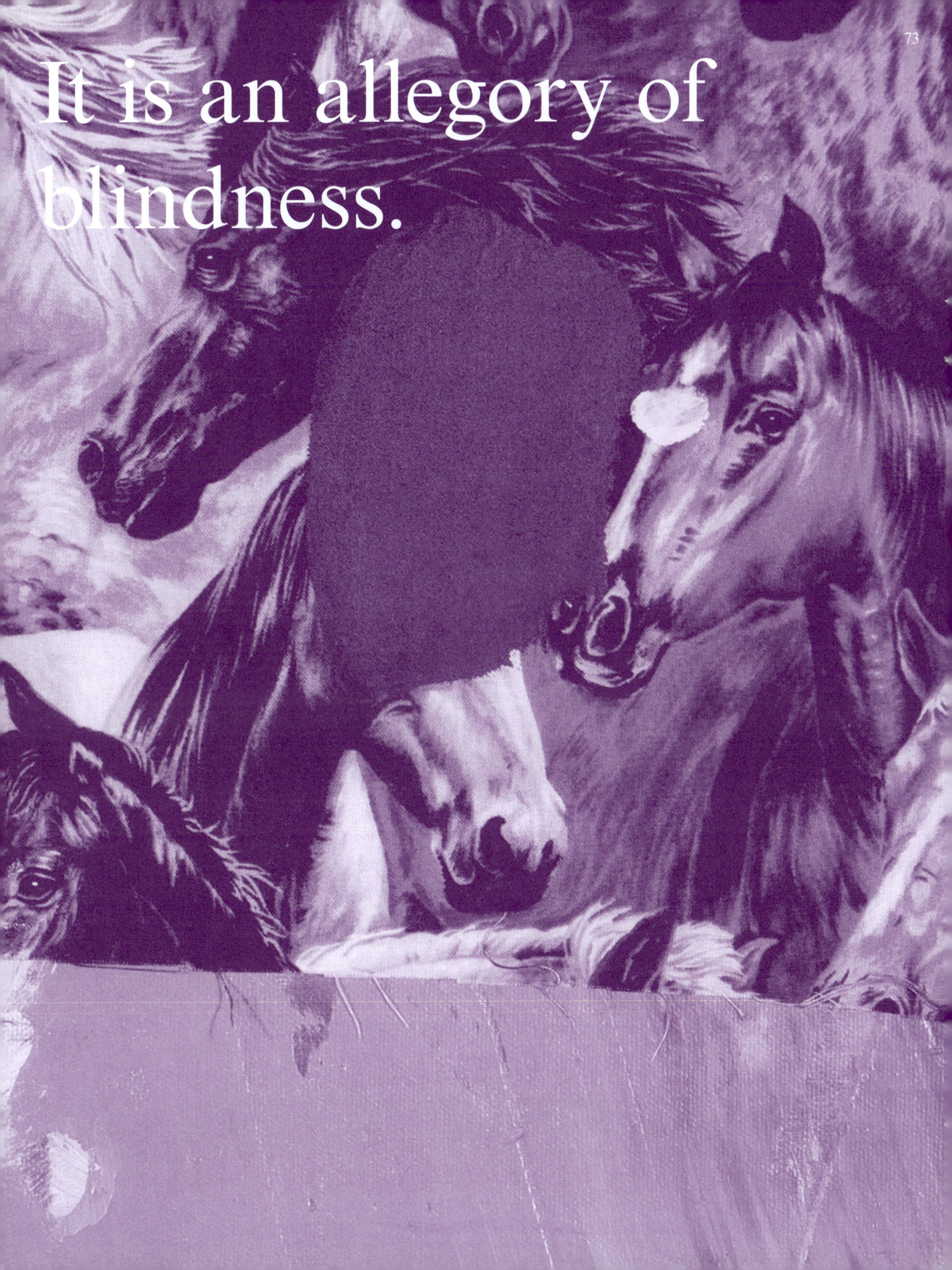
It is an allegory of
blindness.

It is the same allegory as that of the exhibition in general. Painting means to see, but in Mayton's allegory of painting the truth is always drowning, drifting (turning into words, or signs for something else); the triumph of sight

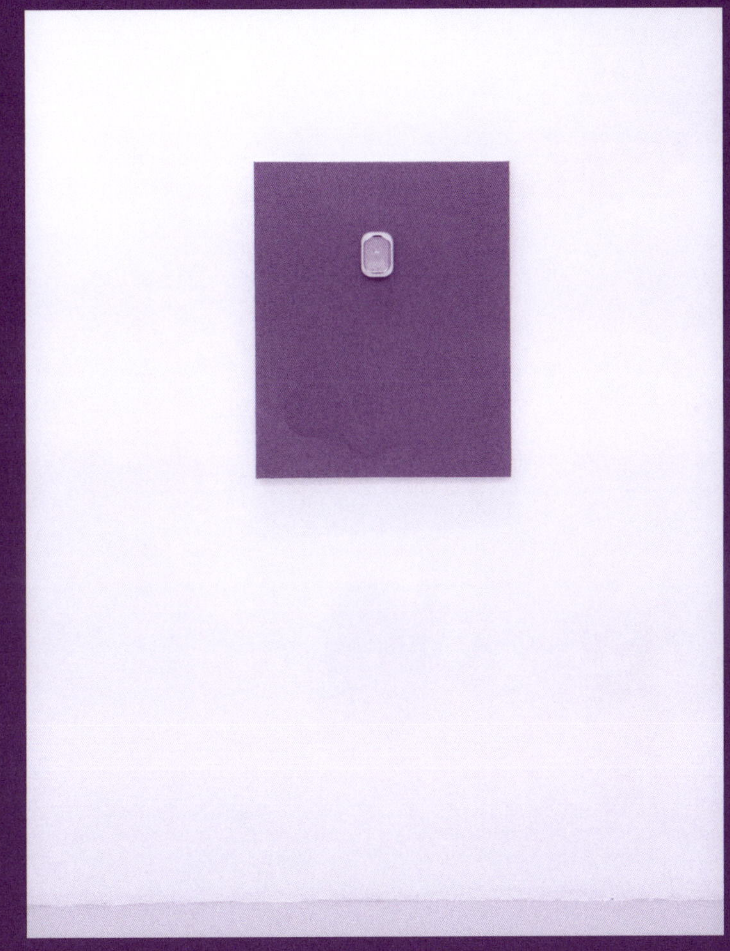

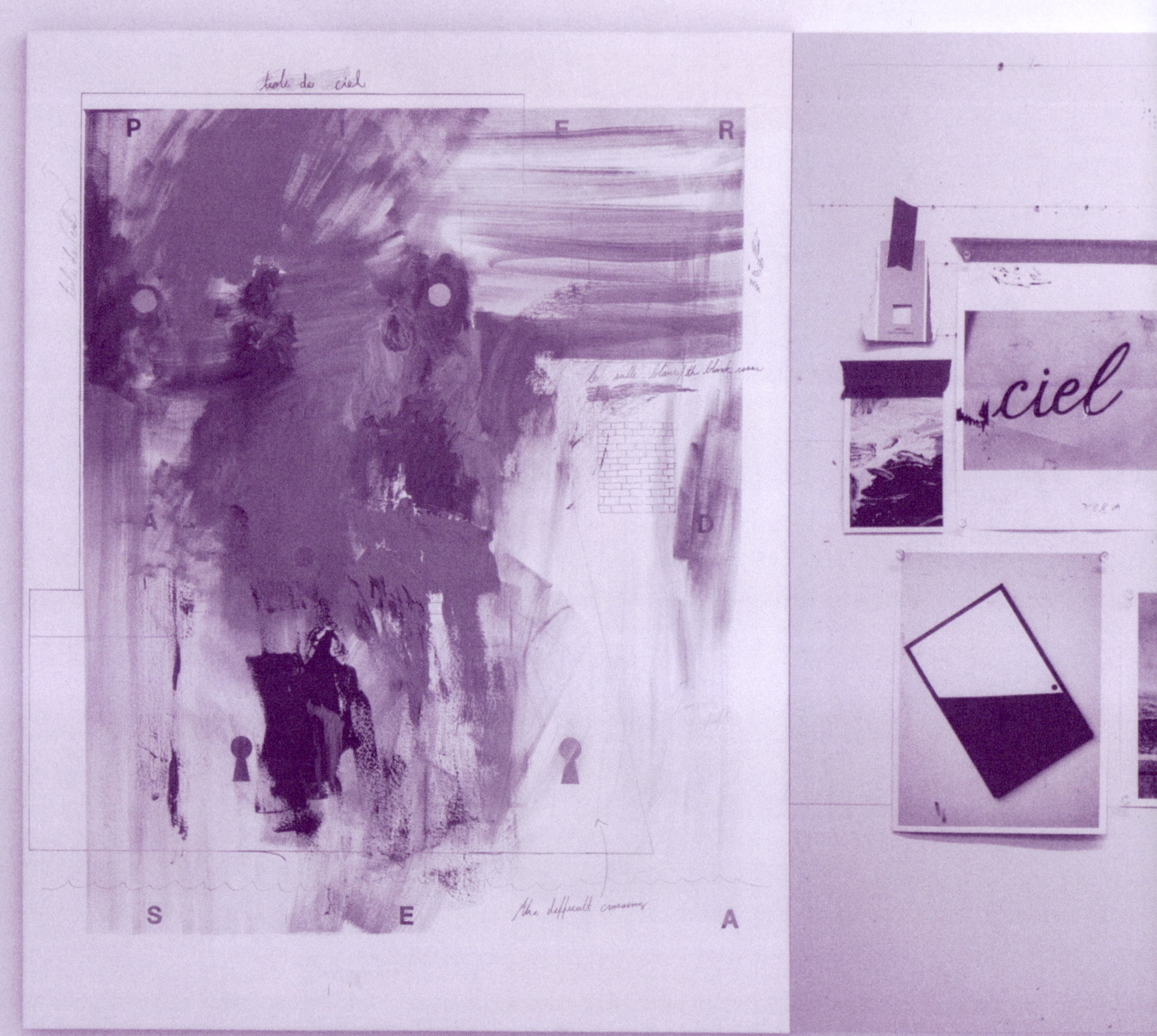
étole de ciel
P   F   R
A   D
S   E   A
the difficult crossings
ciel

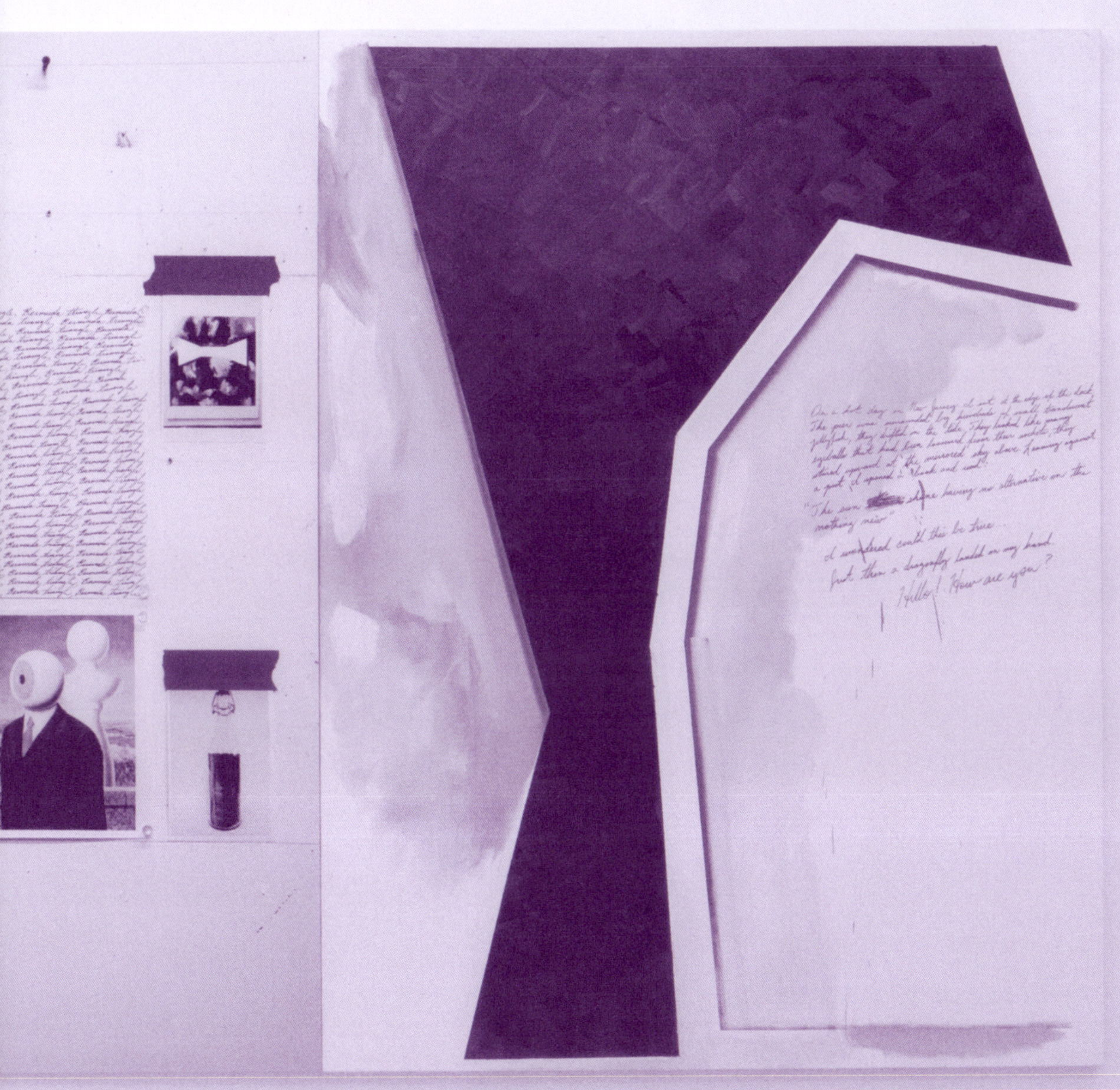

always courts blindness and the cancellation of meaning.

The Rough Sea: Counterargument. But painting is, inevitably, a solar art. The sun, and with it sight, must be the master metaphor of painting. Even in Mayton's painting about blindness and the sea, the sun also rises. Above the words "rough sea" there is a single, tantalizing node of oil paint, the mark of painting's (solar) capacity to proclaim the truth, even under threat of drowning, cancellation, and dissolution. The one depends on the other.

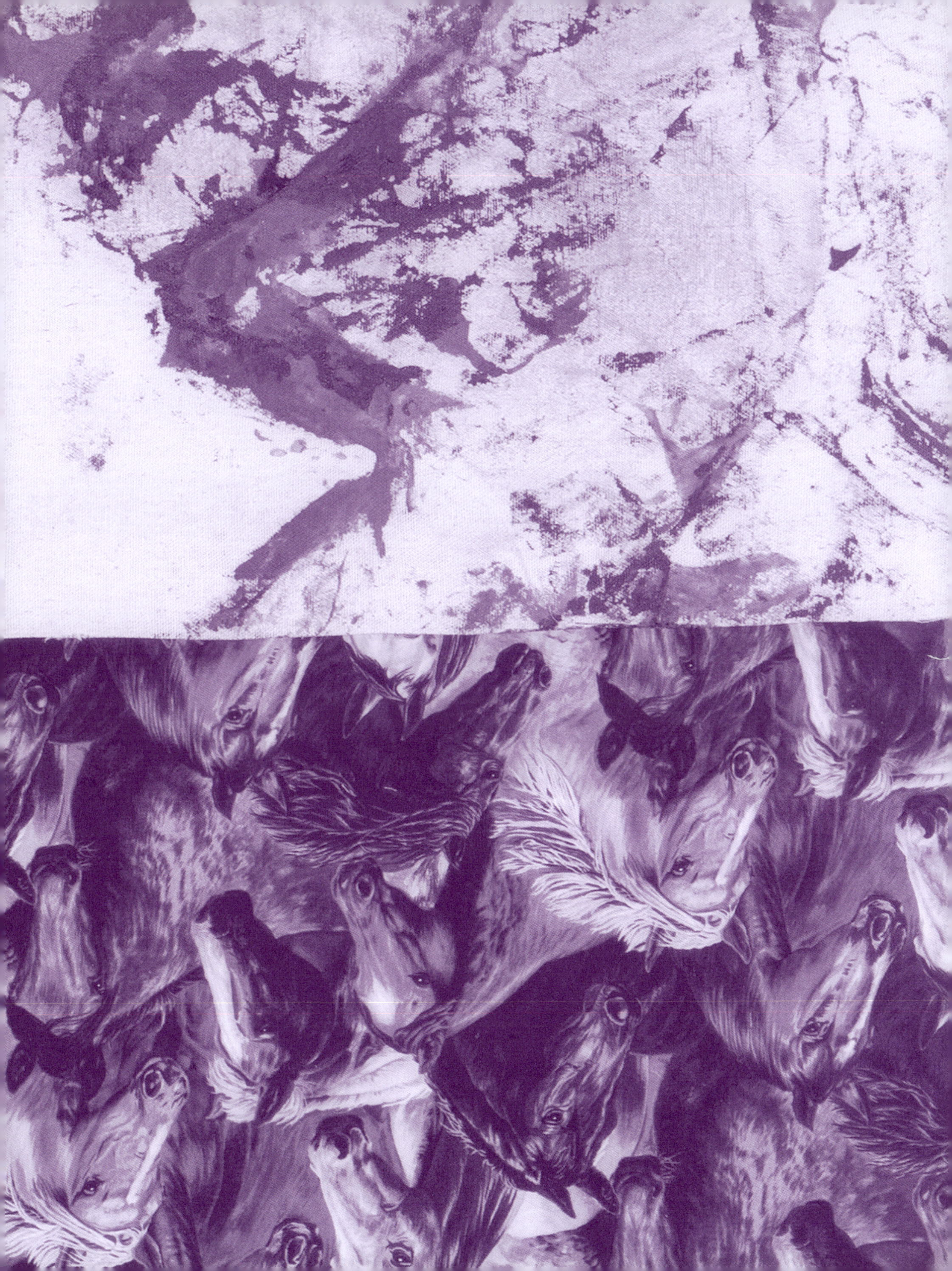

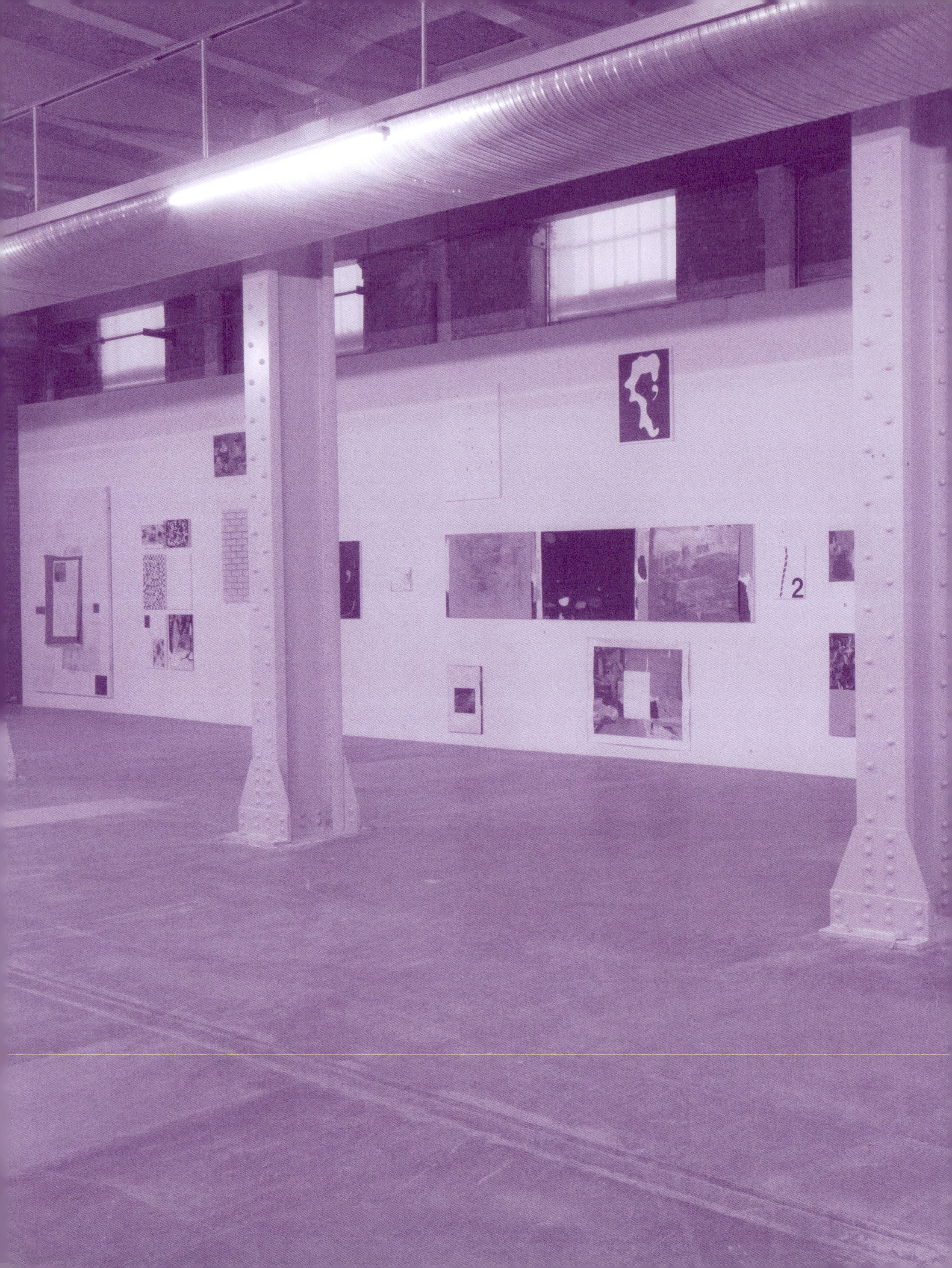

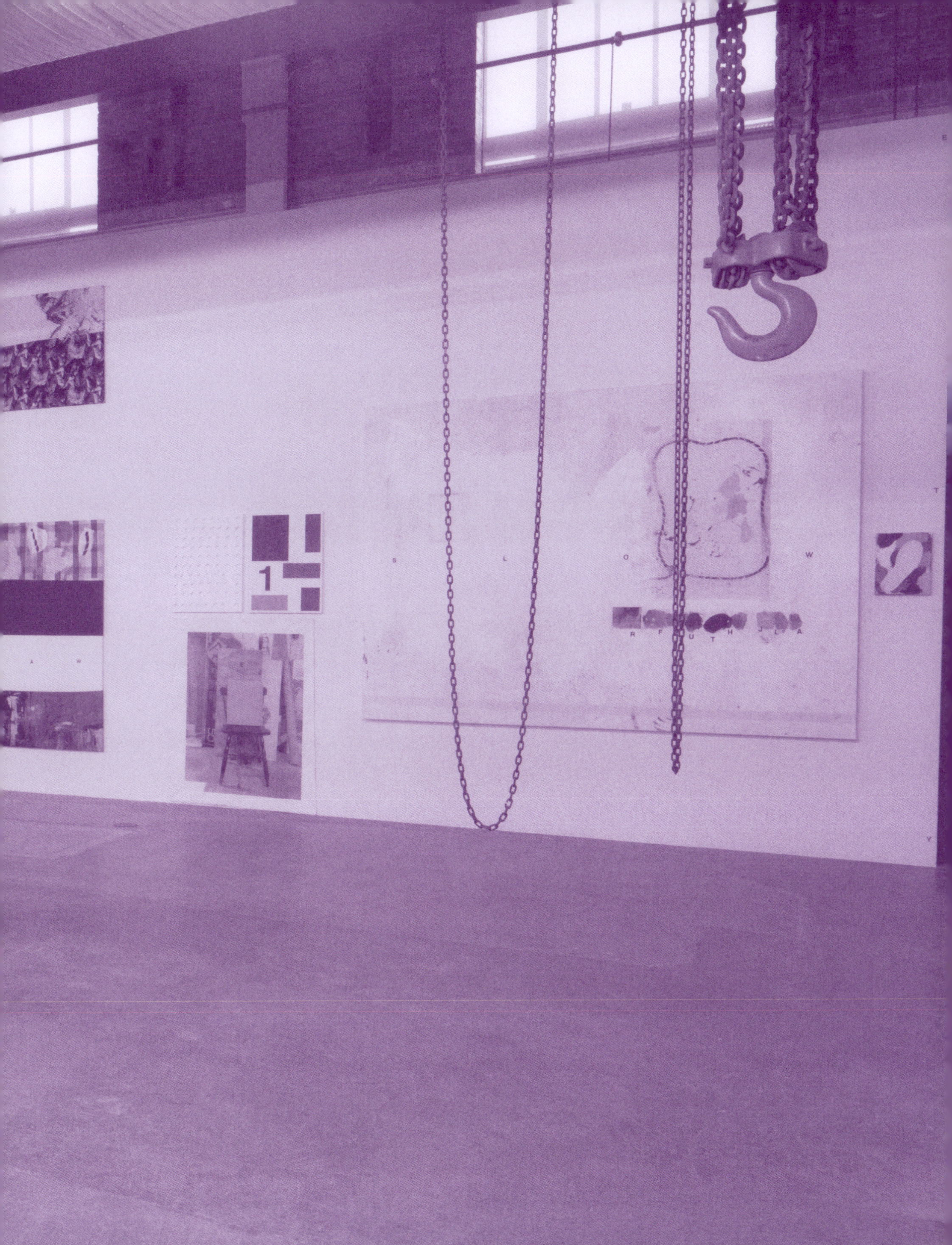

Previous: *Two-Step* at The Power Station, Dallas, 2013

And like a miniature
sun, this nugget of oil
paint—this nugget
of brackish gold—
stains the reversed
photographic paper so
that it looks uncannily
like a halo, or the
suggestion of an icon.

Bodies change.
Signs change.
Meanings change.^{p.128}

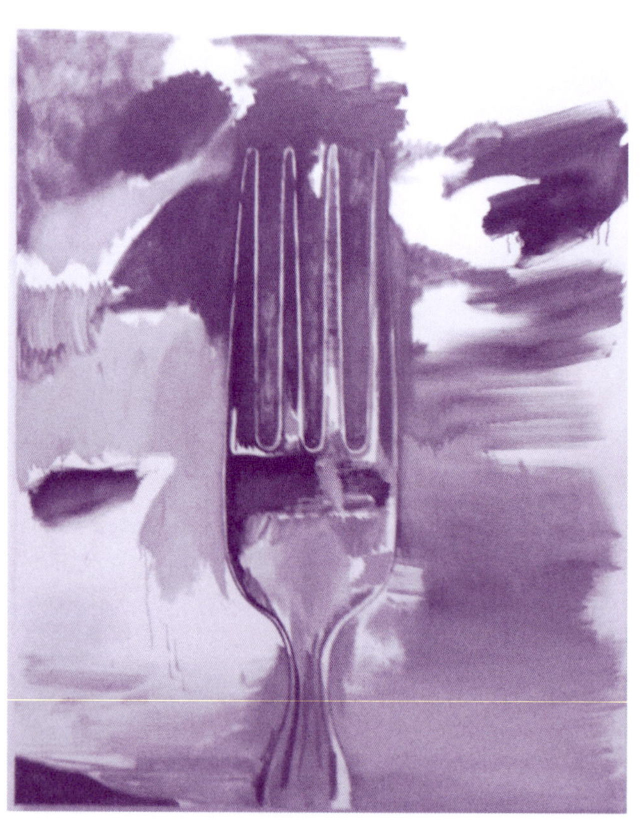

Preliminary conclusion: Robbe-Grillet on Magritte: "A preliminary conclusion is in order: the episode known as *The Difficult Crossing* seems to contain a double allusion to the sinister vessel onto which the adolescent was dragged by her ravagers and to the outrage awaiting her there before she was thrown into the sea. Second (hypothetical) remark: the same wooden, phallomorphic object could have served as a bludgeon for

the young man's accomplices during the ensuing brief struggle ..."

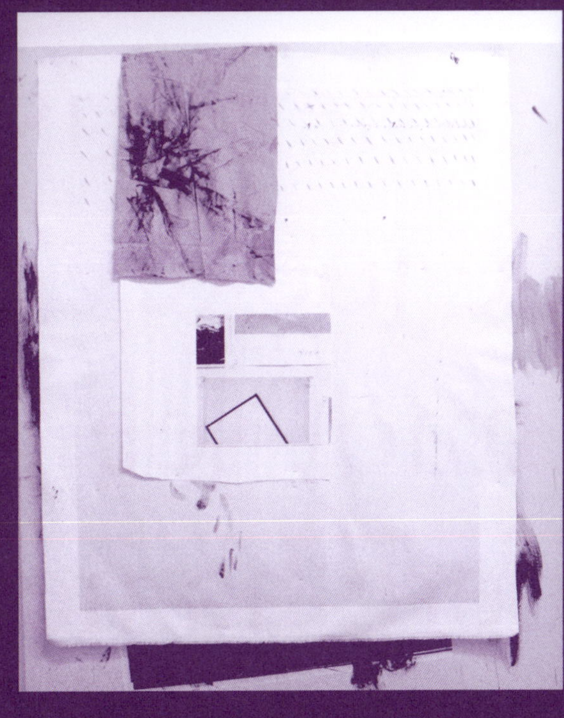

Mayton with (blind to) Magritte—again: The Lost Jockey.^{pp.80–81} The painting refers to Magritte's painting of the same title. Again the theme is blindness. The jockey is lost; he cannot see the way to where he needs to go.

The Painter Dreams the *Mise en Abyme* while Grazing the Unseen Pasture

by Rochelle Goldberg

Order is, at one and the same time, that which is given in things as their inner law, the hidden network that determines the way they confront one another, and also that which has no existence except in the grid created by a glance, an examination, a language; and it is only in the BLANK SPACES of the grid that order manifests itself in depth as though already there, waiting in silence for the moment of its expression.

—Michel Foucault
Les Mots et les Choses

The painted image is well suited to the pursuit of vision, caught and split open as a witness to its own sensory modality—the sense that is self-sensing—the sense that scales a singular mark to corporeal action. Sight to touch, touch to brush, brush to paint, paint to canvas, flips the image back to the eye, another eye, from the painter's space to yours and mine.

Charles Mayton, the painter in question, may not fancy himself a cowboy, but he is guilty of a benign promiscuity that plays out through a short-term, serial crush on the banal motif whose "generic nature leaves room for punctuation" (says Mayton). The materiality of paint facilitates his unique brand of image production, dampening the motif so that the artist can wipe it over any format. For the most part, Mayton's application of paint in service of an image

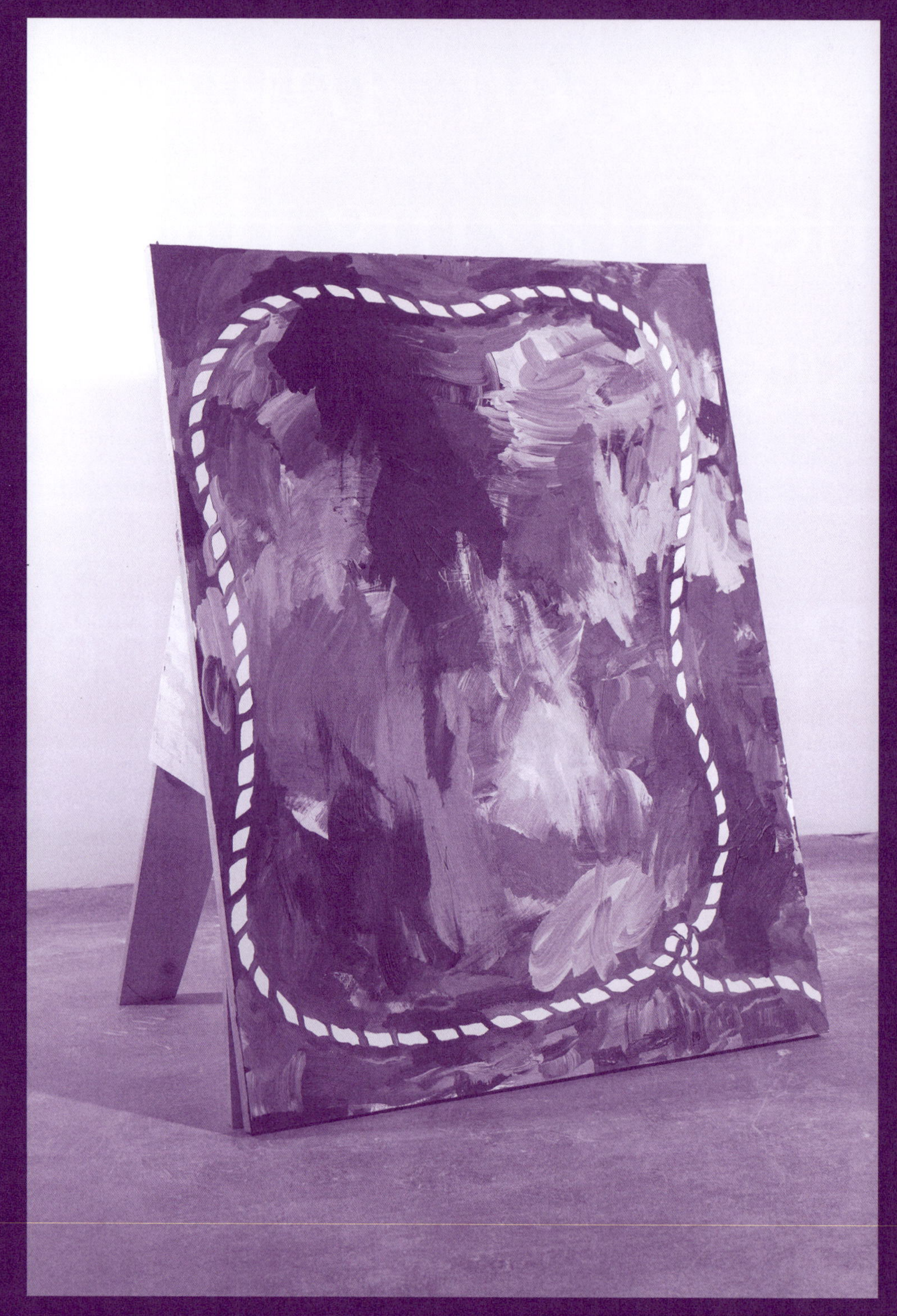

depends on the rectangle as its receptive support, a form that is notably edge on all four sides.

In his recent exhibition *Two-Step* at The Power Station, Dallas, Mayton's lasso, a recurring motif, enters the field as decoy, readying the image for an unknown catch. This expressed desire for the painting to reach outside itself, vision caught as symbolic gesture, is articulated in the *Sawhorse* painting *Figure and Mirage*. Set on the ground and tilted upward, it is practically a trap. The lasso depicted is only present through its absent rendering. A field of colorful marks is omnipresent, while the white rope is bare, defiant. If familiar with the broader trajectory of Mayton's creative output, it is apparent that the intention is a generous offering of guided passage through an unseen pasture, which from here onward will be referred to as the blank space.

The blank is an assertion of empty space. It is expectant. The blank is something we fill, and in filling it, it fills us. A repository for our stare, we blank at it and it blanks back. It echoes our three-dimensionality back to a two-dimensional space that can push all forward, flat and back. This two-dimensional realm has a virtual depth just as reliable as the one we experience in gravitational reality. The blank unleashes itself against planar divisions, obfuscating figure-to-ground relations. In the blank there is no figure and there is no ground. The lasso, the keyhole, the empty plates, and the bow tie are all furthered blanks that then become a cipher for the continued possibility of a zero-degree picture plane that can be opened, suspended, and accessed. The blank is the painter's aim to touch through space, and for space to touch back. In doing so a new space is made.

This new space exists as a compound—a vital archive of everything within and around the painter's eye, my eye, and the painting itself. The blank therefore initiates a chain of visuality that extends outside the parameters of the painted image. This compounding of sight and experience is given concrete expression through the sequencing of other works: an image of the studio, of the gallery space, of the mark, of a can are all drawn out, combined, and presented as the picture we build as vision itself. The canvas becomes a surface to push the archive onto, to hold it in place, so that the relationships of thinking and seeing, thinking about seeing, and seeing without thinking are broken down, made available. It's all in the blank—the unseen pasture.

This pastoral space, the most idyllic scene the painter can depict, is Madonna on the meadow, nothing on the meadow, no meadow, because it is blank. Invisible, but somehow we move into it, move around in it. Although the painting is an extension of everything we already know to be "real," it simultaneously delivers this "real" as an unknown dish—an arena to navigate blindly and feel our way around. Mayton's image anticipates our feeling of it, expects it. The entire space is pre-touched by the brush so that we, too, can then see it. The grass does not have to be real to feel it underfoot, and depending on how it feels we know that it is green.

In *The Venal Muse*, his 2012 exhibition at Balice Hertling, Paris, Mayton presents the blank as a scaling down of the gallery in which the paintings are displayed. The bow tie is simultaneously a simple diagram of the space in which it resides. In the work *The Venal Muse, After René Daniëls*, Mayton references a Daniëls painting that is a reference to the poem of the same name by Charles Baudelaire. In this instance the historic silhouette of the Parisian street walker becomes guide. Walter Benjamin, commenting on Baudelaire's romantic characterization of the prostitute, states: "Thus the eye of the prostitute, scrutinizing passers-by is at the same time on the lookout for the police… [And further quoting Baudelaire] her eyes like those of the wild animal, are fixed on the distant horizon." Her primal stare is self-protective, to look all ways at once while proceeding with caution. The artist's muse has a double function of historical positioning through influence, reference, and the acting out of genealogy, while also acknowledging the value added to the works. The venal muse, a corruptible creative force, because it is available for purchase, performs as a self-reflexive criticism built into the work itself. If obtained, the painting fulfills the role as commodified object through the transaction, but the blank space, an unknown link in the lineage, becomes an exit strategy outside of sustained objectification.

The following text in quotations, written by Mayton, is taken from an email exchange in the lapse between his Paris and Dallas exhibitions.

"There is an answer but it's more of an ongoing question. I never really thought of the blank space until recently. Before it was more about the frame and what happens within its boundaries in a more performative way. I think when I started to think about the blank space it was essentially an open space on which infinite projections could be cast. Not by me as the one to construct the blank but by others that might engage with this openness and thus fill it subjectively. Of course with this comes something like the ( ) or the ' ' or "…," [ ] etc., meaning the context around the blank space is not written directly into it but does allow for suggestive insights to ways that it could be read or filled. So I guess in a way it's not a blank space as much as a gap or a break in what is being presented. As much as I think I am clear in my own work I'm still very aware that much of it, if not most, may probably remain somewhat obscure, which is fine. I suppose some of the 'blankness' might likewise act as measure of this to myself by way of not knowing everything that is being articulated. I'll have to think about this more but maybe something that points to the possibility of a rest in space. I think the unseen pasture is a perfect image for this concept…I thought it was interesting that you used pasture because my mind has been on the landscape or a landscape space since working on this show in Dallas. I assume that it's obvious that things move inward from the open space of the sea to an interior of the land, metaphorically speaking. Wasn't really intended but the context seemed to push the work in that direction."

The blank space has a psychological precedent in the *mise en abyme*.

Imagine the dream:

In a dream you see yourself seeing. The scene is in black and white. You stand in front of a mirror. Standing there in front of the silver surface you watch your eye catch itself. But the I that lies there dreaming, me, is behind the I looking in the mirror. We see both our back and a reflection of the self that stands before us. But the I that conjures the dream, or the I that gazes from behind our self-looking, is not there, is not reflected. We see the dream, but the dream does not see us. The eye that I know is not located in the exchange. And yet, the eyes that catch each other somehow have caught us. After some time the reflection looks through itself right at us, locks with our eye when we are not visibly there. In this moment we split in three. Wake up. The painter is also dreaming.

Dreaming grants access to extended modes of seeing. We creep up behind ourselves. Momentarily standing outside of a situation that we are inevitably a part of. The seeing our self-seeing. This is beyond known reciprocity—a simultaneous face-to-face with the eye seeing and the seeing eye's seeing of seeing. This fictional space of an object splitting informs the thoughts that are rushed toward the canvas. Taking one's time in liminality fuels the impossible into concrete form.

Blanking is an act of indeterminacy. It facilitates a reverberation of location and motif. This action structures the image in resistance to a singular space or temporal event. The blank motif points beyond the line where the image finds its edge, indicating a space that continues infinitely as it is brought back into frame. *Mise en abyme.* An extended space one can never truly catch, where each reflection is partly hidden behind the next. The representation within representation, the image within image, of the display within display within, within, within, an exterior forever internalized, that goes on and on and on. And as simple as the space between two mirrors could never really be. A painting might mark it there.

Mayton:

"Yeah, the blank space. I think you pretty much summed up many of similar thoughts I've had about this. Where does the unseen pasture come from? The use of the word "pasture…" interesting. I'm curious about the blank space as a bridge. In thinking about this now it does have to do with the archive and the notion of holding place, bridging place. I guess the interest has always been place in transition to other spaces, times, voices, etc. In a generic sense we could be talking about frame, but it's complicated by the 'going into' that happens. It's an absorption of substance, being, perception and in the best case scenario the 'blank space' has these qualities of interiority that may or may not be accessible—it does stare back and lure one in. Ok I'm getting a bit lost in this now. It's super late, better come back to this more soon."

Postponed Note:

In Mayton's untitled, unknown and unseen painting that will be nicknamed "The end of the open range is marked by the frame," a layering of images and wiped cloth masks a simultaneity of marks and corners hidden underneath. The painting was made in the temporal/spatial lapse

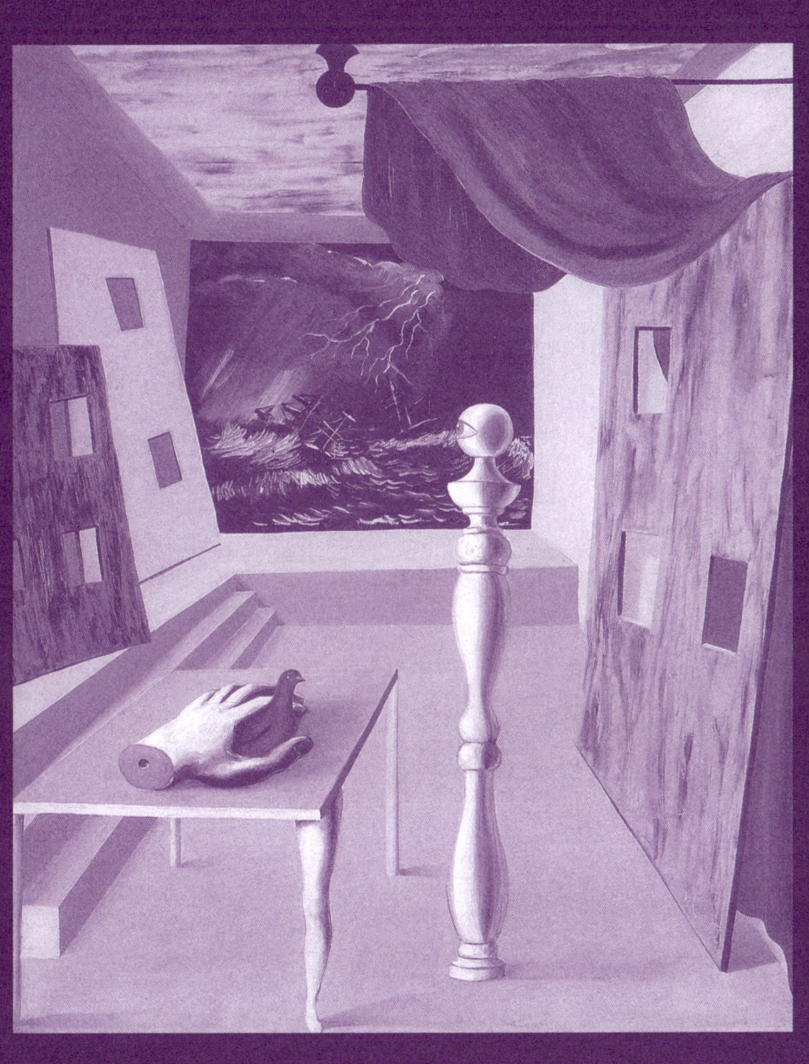

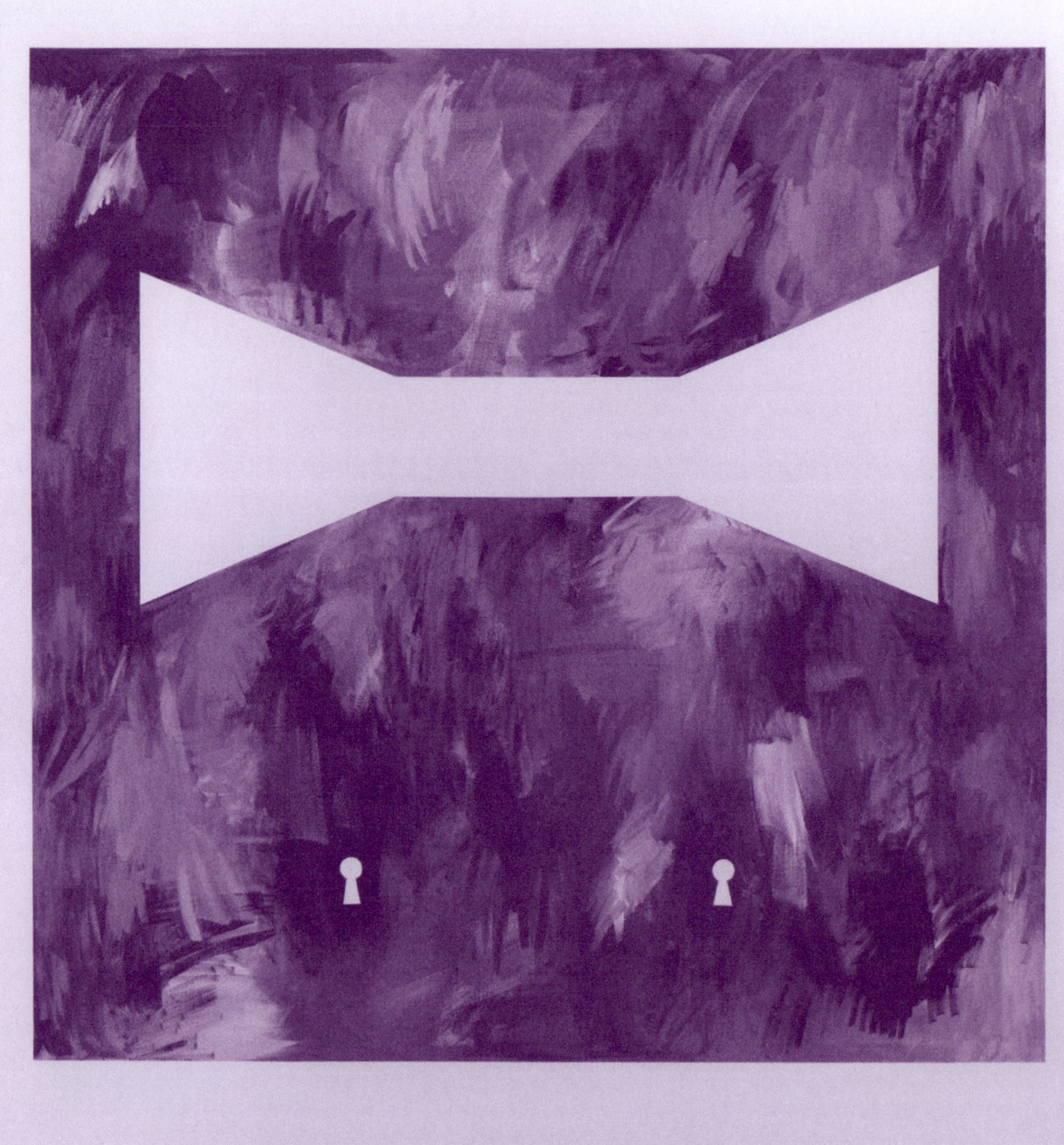

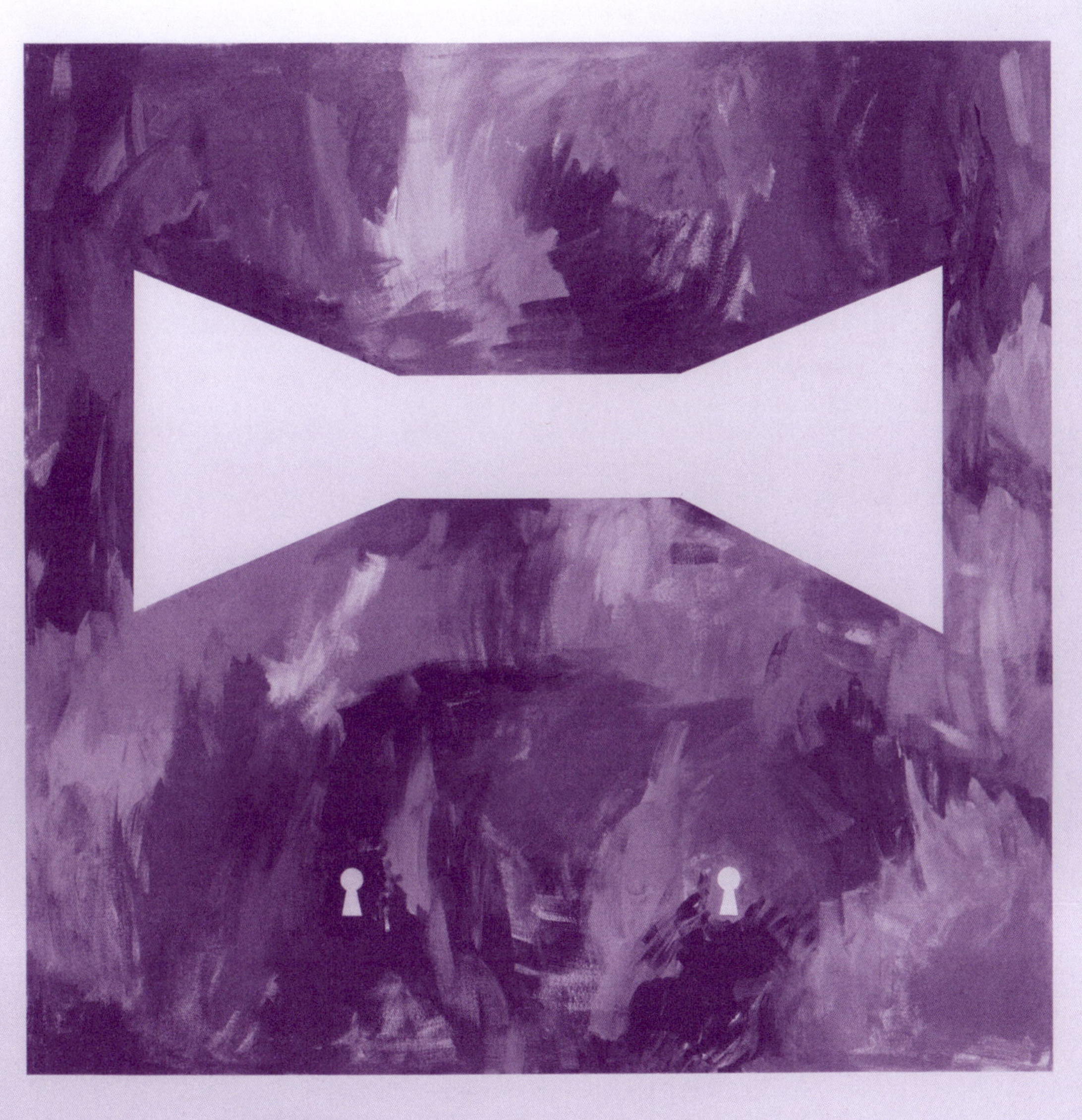

between Mayton's Paris and Dallas exhibitions.
Dislocated between one body and the next, this
piece functions as the generative base place
for a fresh reveal over a lazily covered past.
A cumulative moment is subtly proposed in a
singular glance; the layered exterior ensures the
possibility of an interiority, the coupling of which
is facilitated by the conservation of the frame.

Gesture cropped as rectangle is more than the
concise space for grazing. Rectilinear repetition
enacts a pushing out against an edge that points
back in. The redundancy of the frame facilitates
its reverberation through space and across the
work, wherein the singular edge is amplified as
a multiple threshold. The repeated edge casts
its shadow, creating passage through a divided
plane. Of note is the abandonment of the banal
motif, and in its absence the cowboy presents a
field. Historically, the open range is cut by the
frame to prevent overgrazing the unseen pasture.

The sequel to the dream:

…is the mimetic meltdown. Is the dream with
a memory of the dream built within it. Again
you stand in front of the mirror. Remember the
dream, the glance that connects to a hidden
self behind, to the dreamer. You, the subject
of the dream, direct your attention to your
reflection—a reflection that should be multiple
if you, the dreamer, are seen within it. The eyes
that link pressure a surprising reveal. You do not
know yourself, the dreamer, who reflects behind
the subject you. The reflection denies a self-
actualized dreamer and instead triangulates your
eye with a queue of foreigners in frame. The you
who lies there dreaming, the you who knows you
are there, is merely the memory and a handful of
others. Even if you know the dream, in the dream
it's not yours to call.

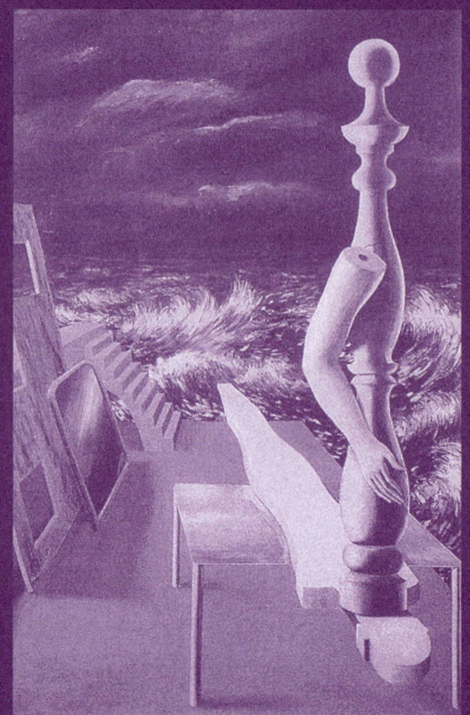

Originally Mayton placed the motif of the jockey in this landscape, but he then painted it out: the lost jockey is himself (literally, materially) lost; the allegory of blindness has itself been rendered illegible or impossible to see.

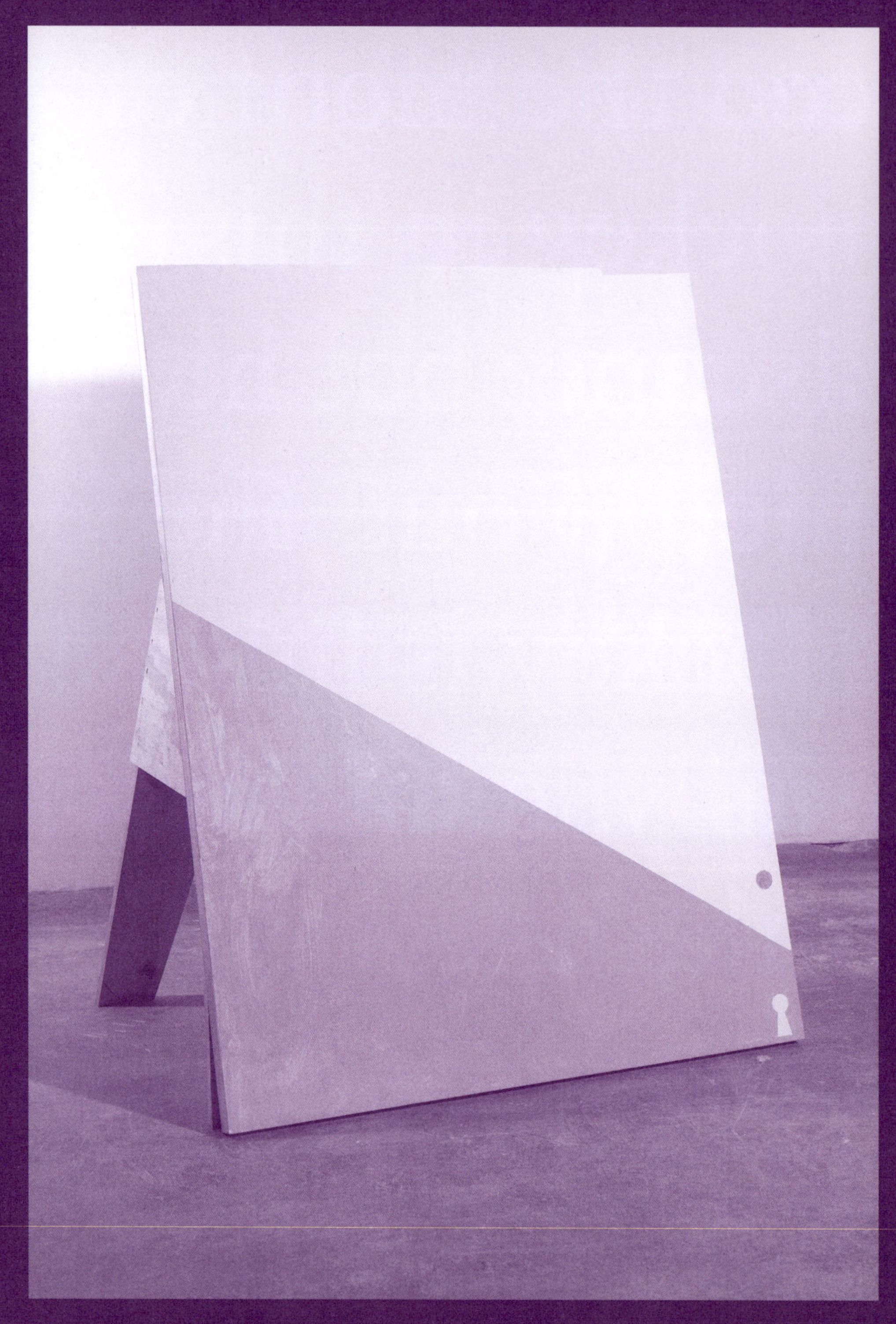

Instead of using motifs to create allegories, here Mayton's paint gobbles up the motif, and in doing so offers an allegory of those motifs: the allegory of (the allegory) of painting.

Strange fate of two dragons. "Dolarhyde falls in love with a blind co-worker named Reba McClane, which conflicts with his homicidal urges. In beginning a relationship with Reba, Dolarhyde starts to consciously resist the

Dragon's 'possession' of him; he goes to the Brooklyn Museum, beats a museum secretary unconscious, and eats the original Blake watercolor of *The Red Dragon*."

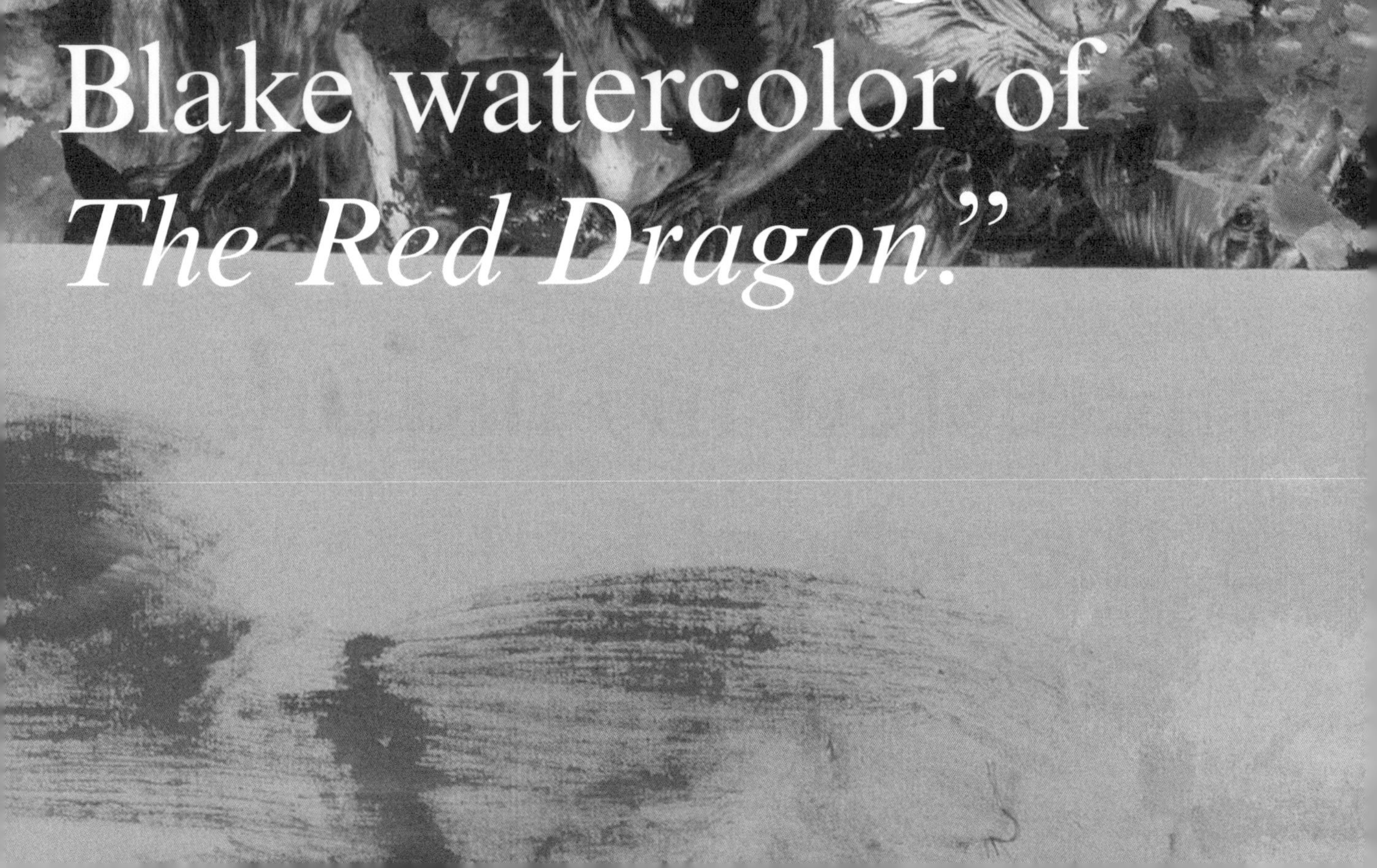

Agnes Martin. Same problem—different solution. "Nature is conquest, possession / eating, sleeping, procreation. It is not aesthetic, not the kind / of inspiration I'm interested in / nature is the wheel […]

You never rest with nature, it's a hungry thing / every animal that you meet is hungry / not that I don't believe in eating / But I just want to make the distinction between / Art and eating."

Robbe-Grillet on Magritte (there's always another fish in the sea): "When you said that the twin Vanessa devours the firebird at the end of the show, what did you mean by that?

It's probably another sexual metaphor, like everything else. If this passage seems superfluous to you, you may eliminate it, even though it represents an interesting inversion of one of the previous episodes: the one with the canned fish."

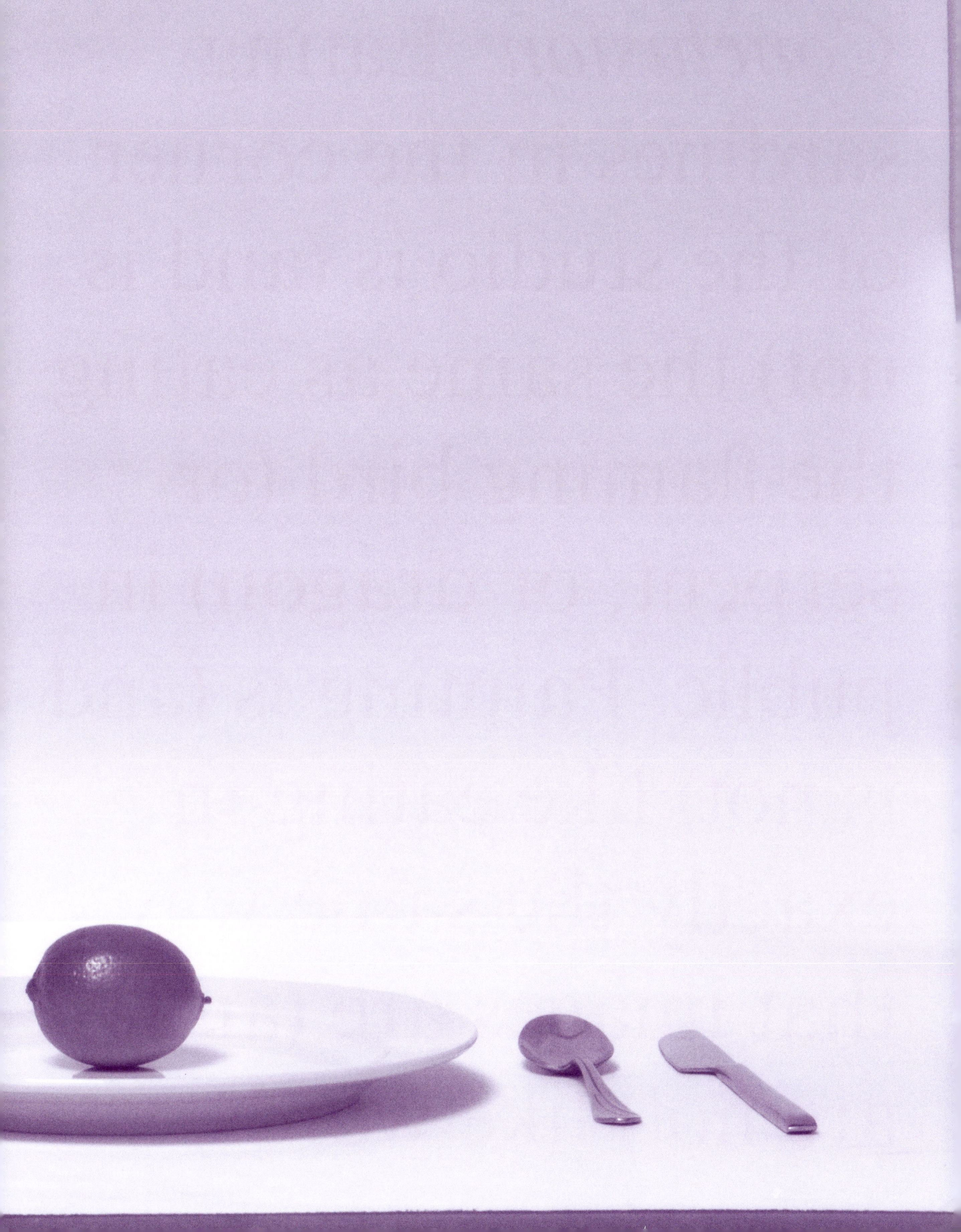

Conclusion: Eating sardines in the corner of the studio is (and is not) the same as eating the flaming bird (or serpent, or dragon) in public. Painting is (and is not) like eating in exactly the same way that images are (and are not) like words.

Coda and recapitulation. Again the sea. Again language. Again language and (as) the sea. Again (or really for the first, and last, time), William Gaddis: "The sea, romantic in books, or dreams or conversation, symbol in poetry, the mother, the last lover, and here it was, none of those things actually before him. Romantic? this heaving, senseless actuality? alive? evil? symbolical? shifting its surfaces in imitation of life over depths of the whole fabric of darkness, of blind life and death. Boundlessly neither yes or no, good nor evil, hope nor fear, pretending to be all these things in the eyes that first beheld it, but unchanged since then, still its own color, heaving with the indifferent hunger of all actuality

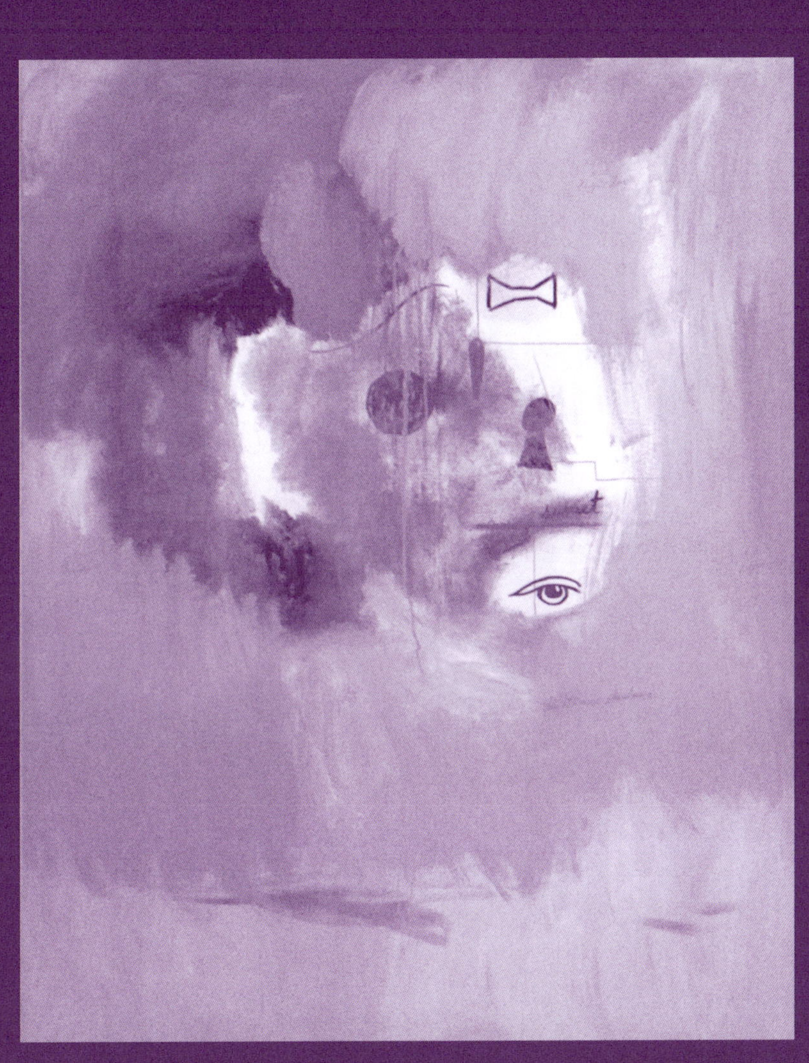

[. . .] The ship heaved, shuddered, dropped its bows on the water. Down below, the white birds finding nothing, startled by the clap of the hull, fled coming up all together, and away, like the fragments of a letter torn up and released into the wind."

Shakespeare:
Full fathom five thy father lies;
Of his bones are coral made;
Those are pearls that were his eyes;
Nothing of him that doth fade,
But doth suffer a sea-change
Into something rich and strange.
Sea-nymphs hourly ring his knell:
Ding-dong.
Hark! now I hear them — Ding-dong, bell.

Credits

1. *Trolling with a Tasteful Palette*, 2012
   Oil on canvas
2. *Somewhere between the Lost Jockey and
   an Unseen Pasture*, 2013
   Gouache on woven canvas
3. *Somewhere between the Lost Jockey and
   an Unseen Pasture*, 2013
   Gouache on woven canvas
4. *the rough sea*, 2011
   Mixed media on panel
5. *S H E W* (detail), 2013
   Acrylic and sewn canvas with oil
6. *Painting Eaten by a Man*, 2012
   Latex and object on canvas
7. *(La traversée difficile) 3–parts*, 2012
   Mixed media on canvas
8. *The Lost Jockey*, 2012
   Acrylic on canvas
9. *S H E W* (detail), 2013
   Acrylic and sewn canvas with oil
10. *Two-Step*, Installation view at
    The Power Station, Dallas, 2013
11. *Untitled*, 2013
    Mixed media on canvas
12. *Figure and Mirage*, 2013
    Acrylic and latex on hollow core door
13. René Magritte, *La traversée difficile*, 1926
    Oil on canvas, 31.5 × 26 inches © 2013
    C. Herscovici, London / Artists Rights
    Society (ARS), New York
14. *The Venal Muse, after René Daniëls*, 2012
    Gouache and oil on canvas
15. René Magritte, *La naissance de l'idole*, 1926
    Oil on canvas, 47 × 31 inches © 2013
    C. Herscovici, London / Artists Rights
    Society (ARS), New York
16. *Figure and Mirage*, 2013
    Acrylic and latex on hollow core door
17. *S H E W* (detail), 2013
    Acrylic and sewn canvas with oil
18. *Tidal wave* (destroyed), 2013
    Oil and mixed media on canvas

The Power Station is a not-for-profit initiative
dedicated to providing a platform for
contemporary art projects in Dallas, Texas.
Housed in a Power & Light building constructed
in 1920, artists are invited to respond to the
raw character of the architecture, offering
an alternative to the traditional gallery
and museum context. Geared toward an
international audience and most immediately
the community of Dallas, the bold programming
serves as a catalyst to provocate public discourse
around art and culture.

Projects and publications at The Power
Station are made possible through funding
provided by The Pinnell Foundation.

The Power Station would like to thank the
following people for their contributions to the
exhibition *Two-Step*: a special thank you to
Rob Teeters, Michael Capio, Rochelle Goldberg,
Blake Rayne, Janelle Pinnell, Greg Ruppe,
Courtney Hamilton and David Lewis.

Design: Front Desk Apparatus
Editing: Rachel Bohan
Printed and Bound by Die Keure, Brugge
Edition: 1,000

Published by The Power Station

The Power Station
3816 Commerce Street
Dallas, TX 75226
www.powerstationdallas.com

Published on the occasion of the exhibition
Two-Step, held at The Power Station, Dallas,
January 19–March 22, 2013.

ISBN: 978-0-9840230-4-2